THE METAPHYSICS OF THE SEXUAL LOVE

THE LIFE OF SCHOPENHAUER

By Ernest Belfort Bax

The great literary exponent of modern Western pessimism, as he is usually deemed, was born in the old Hanseatic town of Dantzic, the 22nd of February, 1788. He was of Dutch descent on both sides. His mother, Johanna Schopenhauer, subsequently became a novelist of considerable, though ephemeral, note. It was by a mere fluke that the subject of our sketch, Arthur Schopenhauer, was not born in England. His father, a Dantzic merchant of considerable means, had all the eighteenth century enthusiasm for English institutions, and the additional connection with Englishmen, which residence in the commercial towns of the Baltic brought with it, especially at that time. He was accordingly anxious that his son should be born on British soil, and to this end undertook a tour with his wife, having London as its goal, in the summer of 1787. Before the time of birth arrived, however, Johanna was seized with a violent longing to return home; and accordingly the future philosopher was ushered into the world, by birth as well an by parentage, a German. The only revenge the old merchant could take upon fate was in the name of his son — Arthur — which was bestowed on account of its cosmopolitan character, at least as regards the three leading nationalities of Western Europe.

In 1793 the old "free town" was annexed by Prussia, a circumstance which involved 'the departure of the Schopenhauers. For father Heinrich Schopenhauer was possessed with great ideas of Hanseatic independence, and the stern municipal republicanism which attached to it. They settled at Hamburg, where Heinrich set up a new business, which he conducted for twelve years. It was here that Arthur Schopenhauer spent his *lehrjahre.* Old Heinrich Schopenhauer destined his son to follow his own calling. In pursuance of this idea young Schopenhauer was educated. In 1797 he was taken by his father to Paris, and subsequently boarded in the house of a merchant of Havre, Grégoire by name, where he remained for two years, being educated in companionship with the son of his host. At the expiration of this time he returned to Hamburg, attending a private school for three years. Schopenhauer junior had, however, never taken kindly to the idea of a mercantile career, and his wishes now definitely turned towards literature, his tastes in this direction being fostered by the literary society he met at his father's house, and to which his mother was greatly addicted. His father, after much entreaty, gave his partial consent, and thought of purchasing a canonry for his son; but the project fell through, and he reverted once more to his original idea, obtaining the son's reluctant acquiescence by the bribe of a lengthened sojourn in France and England, to be enjoyed first.

Early in 1803, accordingly, the family took their departure from Hamburg for Calais and London. While in London, Schopenhauer was placed at the boarding school of a clergyman at Wimbledon. He found the mechanical discipline extremely irksome to him, and, more than all, the religious training imparted in this establishment. There is a passage in one of his letters in which he indicates his disgust, in no measured language, of the atmosphere of cant and hypocrisy which at that time, and for long after, permeated every department of English life, which concludes: "When will the light of truth burn through these darknesses?"

He recurs to the subject several times in the course of his miscellaneous writings, and always in the same strain of inexpressible loathing and contemptuous indignation. At the end of the year the family left England for Paris, touring their route, during the early part of 1804, through provincial France to Switzerland, and ultimately to Vienna. In September young Arthur found his way with his mother alone, his father having gone back to Hamburg, to his native place. Here he entered the office of a Dantzic merchant, and seriously endeavoured to fulfil his pledge to his father at the desk. After a few months, however, he changed the Dantzic office for a Hamburg one; but every month made it more and more apparent that his heart was not in the ledger, the number of moments stolen from business during business hours, in the interest of his books (other than ledgers), were such as to lead to serious remonstrance on the part of his superiors.

Just at this time an event occurred, however, which broke up the Schopenhauer household. On the fifth of April, 1805, his father, who had for some little time previously shown signs of aberration or failing of intellect, was found in the canal, having precipitated himself from the upper story of an overhanging building, the universal suspicion being that the case was one of suicide. This was a great blow to Arthur, who, in spite of their disagreement on the knotty point as to the choice of a profession, was devotedly fond of his father. Though now more or less free to follow his own inclinations, he did not do so immediately, but went back to the drudgery he abhorred, solely, as it would seem, to show his respect for the dead. For two long years he endured it. His mother after a few months — the business complications tending the realization of the effects of her late husband having been settled, and being in consequence possessed of a sufficient income — improved the situation by retiring to Weimar, which was then at its zenith as the literary metropolis of Germany. She here became an associate of the circle which centred in Goethe, and began her career as a novelist. Differences between the mother and son became manifest in the course of correspondence, but did not prevent the former at length giving her consent to a final renunciation of the counting house. At the beginning of 1807, therefore, Schopenhauer began to devote himself seriously to study. In June he settled at Gotha, and, although in his twentieth year, did not disdain to take his place in the *gymnasium* of that town with view to acquiring a thorough classical training. A lampoon on one of the masters compelled his retirement, however, and he went to join his mother at Weimar. In the latter place he pursued his classical studies, but became more than ever estranged from his mother. It soon became impossible for them to live in the same house. Arthur's inadaptability to the somewhat ceremonious etiquette of the Weimar *salon* did not tend to improve matters. The petty spite which only too often displayed itself at a later stage in his gibings at the academical philosophers of his time, at this period found vent in jealousy of the literary renown of his parent. The disgust at the frivolity which was indicated, as it seemed to him, in his mother's conduct, and more especially at the ease with which he thought the memory of his father had been forgotten, no doubt contributed to this; but we must in the main ascribe Schopenhauer's conduct to his constitutional failing. On attaining his majority, and with it the small income of some thousand thalers (£150), Schopenhauer determined to enter the University of Gottingen. He here enrolled himself as a student of medicine, not so much with a view to practising, as for the sake of having a faculty. He attended for over a year most of the classes in physical science. It was nut till some months later that his distinctive leaning towards philosophy showed itself, when he began to attend the lectures of Schulze, the author of "Ænesidemus," and a great man in his day.

Schulze advised him to study Plato and Kant, advice

which he religiously followed for some time, to the neglect of other thinkers. In the summer of 1811 Schopenhauer went to the newly-established University of Berlin; here he attended Schleiermacher's lectures on the History of Philosophy, the following year he also beard Fichte. Already at this time his hatred and jealousy of Academic Philosophy and philosophers began to show itself. Fichte especially came in for his attacks, as may be seen from his student's notebooks of the lectures. These exhibit the silly petulance which too often disfigure his later work. In 1813 came the disastrous campaign of Napoleon in Russia, and the attempt of North Germany to shake off the power of the invader. After the battle of Lutzen Schopenhauer left Berlin, reaching Rudolstadt, a small principality adjoining Weimar. Here he wrote his first book, "The Fourfold Root of the Principle of Sufficient Reason." Its appearance occasioned the joke on the part of his mother, that the title sounded as though it would only interest apothecaries, to which Arthur made the retort, that it would be read when all her romances were forgotten, It was a thin volume, and at the time created no notice. Shortly after the publication, Schopenhauer had the rashness to try the experiment once again of living with his mother at Weimar. This visit proved the occasion of a final rupture with Johanna Schopenhauer, whom he never saw again. At Weimar at this time, however, he entered upon a closer acquaintance or friendship with Goethe than he had done previously. The special occasion of it was his strongly expressed sympathy for Goethe in his squabble with the Newtonians on the subject of the celebrated "theory of colours" *(Farben lehre)*.

Proceeding northward to Dresden, Schopenhauer developed his optical theories as well as his general philosophy in the latter town during the ensuing months. It was here that his pessimism became accentuated and formulated. Schopenhauer claimed to be the first modern who had dealt philosophically with the sexual impulse, which was one of the turning points of his philosophy, the sexual act being the typical illustration of the affirmation of the Will-to-live. But of this more anon, when we come to speak of Schopenhauer's philosophy in general. The belief in the inherent possibility and the practical necessity of a philosophy had already begun to lead him to plan out a coherent system. It was of a different nature from the contemporary academical systems of Fichte, Schelling, and Hegel, in that, while no less than theirs purporting to be a metaphysic, it was nevertheless not like theirs founded on a logical deduction, but claimed to have grown together piece by piece as the fruit of observation and reflection on the phenomena of nature and man. Schopenhauer, in other words, took his stand on a different side of the "critical" philosophy of Kant to that of his contemporaries of the chair. Kant's division of the first part of the "Critique of Pure Reason" into "The Transcendental Æsthetic," and "The Transcendental Dialectic," was the basis of a divergence of view in German philosophy, of which the antithesis between Schopenhauer and Hegel is the most salient expression. While the philosophers of the "chair" took their stand on the Transcendental Analytic and Transcendental Dialectic, Schopenhauer took his on the Transcendental Esthetic. For the former, the formal activity of thought — the category or concept — was the ultimate principle and starting-point of philosophy. With Schopenhauer, on the contrary, this was not ultimate, but derived from the, for him, deeper, non-logical principle of Will. Art thus, in a sense, stood nearer philosophy than science with Schopenhauer. "Art," he writes at this time, "is not, like science, merely concerned with the reasoning powers, but with the innermost nature of man, in which each must count merely for what he is in reality. Now this will be the case with my philosophy, for it is intended to be philosophy as art." .... "The mere faculty of discovering the sequence of conceptions, the combining, in short, of antecedents and consequents, though it may make a great scholar and scientist, will never make a philosopher, just as little as it will make a poet, a painter, or a musician." Schopenhauer was at this time largely occupied with a perusal of the works of the French materialist writers of the last century, especially of Helvétius. The Upanishads in a Latin version also absorbed a good deal of his time, and contributed much material towards his own philosophy. He speaks of it as the noblest reading in the world, and as his highest consolation.

By 1818 the great philosophical work was already all but finished, and Schopenhauer wrote to the publisher Brockhaus, of Leipsic, offering it to him as the exposition of a new philosophical system. Terms were arranged, and an edition of eight hundred copies agreed upon. But Schopenhauer chafed at the delay of the printers, and this finally culminated in the writing of a discourteous and quasi-libellous letter to Brockhaus, demanding a portion of the honorarium, and calling upon him to name a date for the completion of the publication "with all the sincerity of which he was capable." Brockhaus declined to act otherwise than in accordance with the terms of the agreement. He also wrote further letters to Schopenhauer, abusing him in well-set terms for what he deemed his insulting conduct, which letters remained unanswered by the latter. The volume saw the light towards the close of 1818, being dated for the following year, and bearing the title, "The World as Will and Presentment," in four books, with an appendix containing a criticism on the philosophy of Kant. The work proved a failure, as the "Fourfold Root" had done; and Schopenhauer some years afterwards, on demanding an account as to the sale of his book, received a reply that a great part of the edition had been disposed of as waste paper.

Before the book had issued from the press Schopenhauer was in Italy, refreshing himself with the southern sun, after his four years' labour on what he deemed his lifework. It was a time of all others when a re-awakened interest in archaeological research generally, and especially in that of the classical lands, was making itself felt — the time of Niebuhr and of Von Humboldt, of Thorwaldsen and of Bunsen. But Schopenhauer sympathized with none of these. The researches into the origins of Christianity which occupied his college friend at Göttingen, Bunsen, had no attractions for him. Just as little did he care for the new conceptions of history which were dawning, and which found their first expression in Niebuhr's demolition and partial reconstruction of the earlier Roman history. To Schopenhauer, for whom the valley of the Ganges was the one and only original source of the religious instinct, Christianity was unspeakably abhorrent. Historical research was uninteresting to him for the simple reason that he admitted no philosophy of history, no law in history, not even a tendency, but the mere fortuitous play of individual desire and caprice, substantially the same at one time as at another, and differing only in the superficial forms of its manifestation. For classical literature and art, on the other hand, he had a keen enthusiasm, an enthusiasm which had its obverse side in the systematic depreciation of medieval art, especially Gothic architecture. Italy was, just at this time, "the fair land of exiles" from the conventionalities of society in the more northern countries of Europe. Byron, Shelley, Scott, and other lesser lights of English imaginative literature, were languishing, rhapsodizing, or sight-seeing in Venice, Florence, Rome, and elsewhere. Goethe had only recently been there, and there were plenty of other Germans, intoxicated with the "romantic " movement now springing into life, with whom Schopenhauer had the opportunity of quarrelling. He kept a diary during all this time, in which were set down sundry reflections on life and things of the partly platitudinary and partly paradoxical nature, so characteristic of all the meditations of our Neo-Buddhist on things in general.

At Naples he received a letter from his only sister, who was a few years his junior, containing a report of the publication of his book, and also the welcome information that Goethe, in spite of his general repulsion to purely speculative literature, had dipped into it, and discovered two passages to his liking, one in the fourth part, which contained Schopenhauer's views on art, and the other a passage in which he proclaims self-realization as the end of life. While at Milan, on his return home, a less welcome letter from his sister reached him, containing the information that the Dantzic house, in which his mother and sister had invested their means, had failed. Schopenhauer, who was himself involved to the extent of 8,000 thalers in the affair, was at first sympathetic, and prepared to stand by his relatives. But on hearing that they had precipitately agreed to accept the first offer made, of a composition of thirty per cent., he became disgusted, and not even the satisfaction he might have derived from seeing therein a confirmation of his theories as to the business incapacity of women, sufficed to prevent an enduring rupture. He himself resolutely stuck to his guns, refusing anything less than seventy per cent down in settlement of claims. This he communicated to the firm indicated, in a letter, in which he states it to be his duty to defend his patrimony, at the same time justifying his attitude on quasi-philosophical grounds. He did not oppose the action of the other creditors, and hence the agreement with them was signed in the summer of 1821. The following month he sent in the first of his acceptances, and in less than a year all his three bills were paid up with interest. The amount gained or saved by his dexterous manipulation was partially lost afterwards, however, through an unlucky investment in Mexican Bonds.

Schopenhauer next went to Heidelberg, and from thence to Dresden to arrange his affairs, the hope inspiring him all the time of obtaining a university appointment. Just now the universities were regarded by the governments of Germany, in the full flood of the reaction represented by the Holy Alliance, as hotbeds of sedition. This made little difference to Schopenhauer, whose want of appreciation of history was only equalled by his contempt for politics and all public movements. For him the individual was all in all. The political atmosphere therefore was no hindrance to his applying, as he hoped with success, for a post of the kind. He first turned his attention to Berlin, and in writing to one of the professors there on the subject, he declares that what interests him alone are the things which concern every man at all times and in all places, and that so long as he has the means and opportunity of study, and of elaborating his ideas and communicating them to the world, he is satisfied, no matter what the outward circumstances of his age and country may be. To Berlin accordingly he went, and after the usual formalities — presentation of copies of his books, a lecture delivered before the Senate, followed by an oral examination — he was admitted to the post of *privat-docent* or extraordinary professor. Thus empowered, in the summer semester of 1820 he began a course of lectures on philosophy. This, like his books, proved a complete and utter failure; his audience dwindled to nothing before the end of the term, and Schopenhauer never again tried his luck in this direction. He was perhaps partly himself to blame for the so completely disastrous collapse of his scheme, inasmuch as he had tried conclusions with the great philosophical giant who was then at the height of his renown. Schopenhauer was literally crushed beneath the weight of Hegel. The former had had the temerity to choose the lecture hour of his famous colleague for his own course. From this time forward dates the bitter and malignant attitude of Schopenhauer towards the great master of speculative thought. The silly ebullitions of spite which recur again and again, in season and out of season, marring the pages of Schopenhauer's Essays, and more than one specimen of which will be found in the following pages, are so puerile as to excite nothing else than pity for the man of unquestionable power who could descend to them. It is only fair to say that Schopenhauer, possessed as he was with a morbid mania of suspicion, probably really believed his failure to have been due to the machinations of his arch-enemy, as he considered the author of the "Phaemomenologie." As a matter of fact it is extremely improbable that Hegel ever once gave so much as a passing thought to the obscure *privat-docent* and his course, so far as jealousy was concerned.

A review of his book in the "Litterateur-zeitung" of Jena next drew Schopenhauer into a furious squabble with the editor. In the course of the year 1821 he fell into a dispute subsequently ending in an unsuccessful litigation, this time not with any academical or literary opponent, but with a friend of his landlady. He complained to the latter on one occasion of having found three strange women conversing immediately outside the two rooms he occupied, and received the assurance that such a thing should not occur again. A few days afterwards, on returning home from his walk, he found the three women again in the same position. He ordered them to retire, but one of them, a seamstress, who occupied a room at the top of the stairs, refused. Schopenhauer thereupon went back into his room, and after waiting a few minutes returned to the charge, and finding her still in the same position, he seized her by the waist and violently flung her out, at the same time using an expression more energetic than parliamentary, and following up her ejection by flinging after her the work she was engaged on, together with the implements of her calling. The case, which came into court, and was defended by Schopenhauer himself, was decided in his favour after the lapse of some months. The plaintiff however appealed, and Schopenhauer, who wished to get away to Switzerland and Italy, did not stop for the hearing, and was condemned undefended to a moderate fine. After being absent in Italy during the whole winter, he returned northwards, making a lengthened stay at Gastein, and in August he was back at Dresden, remaining there some eighteen months, and occupying himself the while with sundry literary projects, including a translation of Hume's philosophical works, albeit this never got beyond the preface. In the spring of 1825 he was recalled to Berlin to square accounts with the redoubtable spinster, who had recently set up a fresh claim against him, on the ground of permanent disablement from gaining her livelihood, having been a consequence of the assault committed three years previously. She now demanded a regular yearly allowance as indemnity. The case had gone against him, and the previous October he had been condemned in costs, and ordered to pay the woman fifteen thalers a quarter (about £9 a year) towards her maintenance. His immediate object in going to Berlin now was to get the verdict reversed. In this he was unsuccessful, and after some months of litigious vexation the decree was made final in March of the following year. The woman herself, who was over fifty years of age at the time, might have furnished Schopenhauer with the theme for a dissertation on the toughness of constitution possessed by the sex, or as he might have put it, on the strength of the manifestation of "The Will-to-live" enshrined in the female body. Among other illnesses, she was prostrated by the cholera when it appeared in North Germany a few years later, and while strong men around her were succumbing in some cases to what were apparently much lighter attacks, she recovered, and survived for many a long year to enjoy the receipt of the pension allotted to her by the law. But last of all this woman died also, and on receiving official information of the fact, Schopenhauer inscribed on the notice-paper the significant and appropriate words, *Obit anus abit onus.*

Schopenhauer continued, notwithstanding his defeat in the law-courts, to reside in Berlin for some years, leading a solitary life, a favourite dog (he was devotedly attached to animals) his only companion. He dined regularly at the table d'hôte of the Hotel de Russie, music and the drama forming his chief relaxations during the time. Among various other literary projects, he entertained an idea of translating Kant's "Critique of Pure Reason," "Prolegomena," and "Critique of Judgment" into English, his knowledge of which language was perfect. This too, however, after the passage of sundry letters between Berlin and London, fell to the ground. In the summer of 1831 the cholera appeared in Berlin, one of its victims being, as is well known, Schopenhauer's great rival Hegel. Schopenhauer, who had a constitutional horror and terror of infection, fled precipitately from the capital on the approach of the enemy, and sought refuge in Frankfort-on-the-Maine, which he never again quitted for any length of time so long as he lived. Our thinker, who had a distinctly superstitious vein in him, which, moreover, in no way conflicted with his philosophy, believed himself warned in a dream that he should die of cholera if he remained.

On his arrival in Frankfort a feeling of isolation, and consequent melancholy, owing to the sudden change from familiar scenes, induced him to renew a correspondence with his sister. Both mother and daughter had now quitted Weimar, and Adele — such was the name of the sister — had taken, like her mother, to the production of light literature. But though a desultory correspondence was resumed, he nonetheless remained estranged as before from his two relatives as far as personal intercourse was concerned. The next year, 1832, Schopenhauer removed for a few months to Mannheim, which for some reason he thought he should prefer to Frankfort as a place of residence. The change, however, proved not to his liking, and he returned to Frankfort. Among his remains were found an accurately drawn up *pro* and *contra* account respecting the two places, in which Frankfort wins because of its greater life and facility of amusement, its able dentists and "less bad physicians," and last, but not least, its "more Englishmen." This, like many other of the memoranda and notes of Schopenhauer, is written in the English language. His life work henceforward was amplifying, commentating on, and illustrating his philosophy as embodied in his "chief work," as he is fond of terming it. In his philosophy, as he repeatedly says, he found occupation, instruction, and recreation — the fullness of life — in short, his happiness, in so far as such was possible to him.

For years his daily round was a perfectly regular one. He rose at half-past seven, took his bath, at that time a rare luxury in Germany, dressed, prepared and drank his coffee, gave instructions to his housekeeper not to interrupt him till noon, and settled down to three or four hours' work, which, he considered enough for continuous intellectual application, whether in reading or writing. At twelve o'clock he knocked off, took a turn at practising on his flute, and at one o'clock dined at his hotel, which was at first the "Englischerhof," and in later years the hotel "Zum Schwann." He seldom talked during or after dinner, except when an especially cultivated or appreciative guest happened to be sitting beside him. After dinner he returned to his domicile, took his coffee, and slept for an hour. He then read *belles lettres* till four o'clock, being widely versed in English and French novelists. At four, or a little after, Schopenhauer started for his constitutional, accompanied by his dog. There had been a succession of these dogs, mostly poodles, since his student days. The poodle used to be called by the children of the neighborhood *young Schopenhauer.* Occasionally, though rarely, an acquaintance took part in these strolls. The philosopher walked rapidly, so rapidly that few could keep up with him, for two hours on end. When alone, he often stopped suddenly for a moment, if an idea struck him, in order to note it down. On his return at six o'clock, or thereabouts, he visited the reading-room, where he regularly perused "The Times." At half-past eight he took his supper, which consisted of a cold collation and half a bottle of light wine. He then lit his long German pipe, and read for an hour. Directly after he went to bed, always believing in a long night's rest. To the obvious taunt which might have been applied to him that he did not carry out his own ascetic ideal, he would have replied that this could with no more reason be required of the philosopher than of any other man. If the philosopher by his insight could intellectually grasp the ideal of life and set it down in theory, this did not imply any greater obligation to realize it in his own person than in the case of anyone else. He who drives fat oxen need not himself be fat. The sculptor who produces a beautiful form may himself be a Silenus. And conversely, we do not expect an Adonis, just because he is an Adonis, to Le also a Phidias.

Schopenhauer published in 1836 a small volume on "Will in Nature." This was his first literary production of any consequence since the completion of "The World as Will and Presentment" in 1818. In it he collected various recently discovered facts of physical science that he thought corroborated the central positions of his philosophy, which he always contended could be arrived at by an inductive process. The new work, like its predecessors, failed to arrest, much less to secure, public attention. He was much disgusted at being known as the son of the novelist Johanna Schopenhauer, rather than as the author of the great philosophical system which should for ever solve the riddle of life. In 1838 a learned society at Drontheim, in Norway, offered a prize for the best essay on the question, "Whether the freedom of the Will could be proved on the testimony of consciousness?" Schopenhauer at once competed, and early in the following year he received intimation that his essay had won the prize. His delight at having, after so many failures, at last secured a measure of success, if not with the greater public, at least with a learned body like the Swedish Academy, knew no bounds. So elated was he, that he at once set about competing for another prize for an essay on "The Foundations of Morality," which had been offered the previous year by the Royal Danish Academy of Copenhagen. The essay having been duly finished and sent in, its author confidently awaited the news of a second success, and was intensely disgusted when he was apprized of the fact that his work had been rejected on the grounds that it contained no adequate discussion of the relation of metaphysics to ethics; that the alleged proofs of sympathy being the Foundation of Morality were insufficient; and lastly, which was worst of all, that eminent philosophers had been treated without due respect. Who these philosophers referred to were may be imagined. Fichte, Schelling, and Hegel became more than ever the incarnation, for him, of deceit, sophistry, and low conspiracy to ignore him. The existent professors of philosophy, who had mostly drunk at these fountain heads, were carrying on, he was sure, the work of the arch-villain Hegel. Both treatises were published in one volume in 1841, at Frankfort, with the title "The Two Fundamental Problems of Ethics." Three years after this the second edition of "The World as Will and Presentment" was issued from the press, without *much* change, except in the appendix on the Kantian philosophy, where his views on the relative merits of the first and second editions of the "Critique" were for the first time set forth. The important new feature was the addition of a commentary on the whole in the form of a second volume, which actually exceeded the first in bulk.

The days of 1848 brought Schopenhauer's anti-political and anti-social side into prominence. He was desperately frightened lest he should lose his means in a general overturn. His essentially individualist impulses, and his views as to the functions of the "superior person" in the economy of human life, naturally led him to hate the populace — the *sovereign canaille,* as he called it. He saw from his window the erection of barricades on the bridge over the Maine, and his roam was on one occasion used by a party of Austrian troops as a citadel from which to open fire on the insurgents in the street below. The disturbance in the even tenor of his life, caused by the events of the revolution, naturally intensified Schopenhauer's bitterness towards it; for an egoist he was and remained, from first to last. We are not surprised, therefore, that he left a large part of his fortune to the surviving relatives of those who fell on the reactionary side. The general break-up, however, of the previous conditions of German life, both material and intellectual, of which the revolution of 1848 was an indication, told in favour of Schopenhauer's literary claims. Disciples and admirers now began gradually to drop in. First of all came the old "councillor" of Magdeburg, Dorguth by name, who was the earliest to call public attention to Schopenhauer in an exaggerated estimate of his claims, embodied in a pamphlet, the first of a series in the same style which ran on up to Dorguth's death in 1854. More important was the acquisition of the popular writer on philosophical subjects, Julius Frauenstädt. The latter became the most useful and enthusiastic exponent of Schopenhauer's views, as well as for many years his adviser in practical matters relating to publishing, etc. In newspaper and review Frauenstädt was untiring in asserting his master's claims to recognition, and in expounding and defending his philosophical positions. His chief literary work in this connection was his "Letters on Schopenhauer's Philosophy." But Schopenhauer, now advancing to old age, was more than ever difficult to get on with; and a rupture of three years in the personal relations between master and disciple occurred, which was only terminated a few months before the death of the former. Adam von Doss, a Bavarian lawyer, also entered upon a vigorous correspondence with Schopenhauer. Lintner, the assistant editor of the "Vossische Zeitung," was converted by a perusal of the "Parerga," and paid especial attention to the theory of music contained in Schopenhauer's system. He also collaborated with Frauenstädt, after Schopenhauer's death, in a work, the main object of which was to defend the personal character of the master against aspersions which had been thrown upon it. In 1853 the well-known article of John Oxenford, the English dramatic critic, entitled "Iconoclasm in German Philosophy," was published in the "Westminster Review," and Schopenhauer was for the first time introduced to the British public. Other friends there were whom Schopenhauer won, the most important being Dr. David Asher, who was attracted by the pessimist's musical speculations while, a teacher at Leipsic, and who subsequently became connected with the publishing firm of his name; and last, but not least, his biographer, Dr. Gwinner.

It was the "Parerga and Paralipomena," which was published in 1851, that first gave Schopenhauer a reputation with the general public. This, his last important work, was the first to attain any immediate success. It was nevertheless declined at the outset by three publishers in succession, and, as it was, his only payment for the copyright consisted in a dozen copies of the book. The strange conglomeration of literary odds and ends on things in general "caught on" almost at once, and led to a republication of the essay on "Will in Nature"; to a third edition of "The World as Will and Presentment"; and shortly before his death, in 1860, to a re-issue of "The Two Fundamental Problems of Ethics." Schopenhauer's chief pleasure in his old age now became reading favourable notices of his own works. His appetite for public applause was voracious. Admirers were frequently attracted to the new philosophy by special points. To some it was his musical theories; to others, those on sexual love; to others, again, his views on mesmerism and hypnotism. But the incoming throng of adherents, admirers, and interested readers was almost entirely composed of the class known as "persons of general culture." The Universities still remained closed to him, and few of those specially trained in them took any interest in the new pessimism or its exponent. One day he received a visit from an officer stationed at Magdeburg, who informed him of the existence of a society of admirers among the military of that city. The officer stated that he himself had read nothing else but Schopenhauer for the past three years. In fact, in the last few years of his life, Schopenhauer had become a celebrity whom the curious passing through Frankfort desired to see. In 1855 he sat for his portrait to a French painter. The next year he was painted by a German artist, a native of Frankfort, while a little later his bust was modeled by a young lady artist of Berlin. Still the evidences he obtained of his renown did not keep pace with his vanity. He could never read enough about himself. He repeatedly laments that so much that had been written about him mint be escaping his notice. The first indication of any academic interest in him was furnished by the University of Leipsic, which in 1857 offered a prize for the best critical essay on his system. About this time Schopenhauer saw his friend Bunsen for the last time. The short visit the latter paid to Frankfort seems to have been the occasion of a pleasant revival for both parties of old student memories. The summer of 1860 showed considerable evidences of the results of old age. Schopenhauer's strong constitution no longer stood him in good stead. Palpitation of the heart forced him to modify his constitutionals. An attack of inflammation of the lungs, from which he but slowly recovered, left him for a long time prostrate. Recurrent seizures of faintness seemed to indicate something radically wrong with his heart. Finally, on the morning of the 21st of September, 1860, after having risen and partaken of his breakfast as usual, he was found lying back dead on the sofa by his medical attendant, who had come to pay what for some time now had been his regular morning visit.

Schopenhauer has attracted as much interest by his personality as by his writings. As is sufficiently obvious, his was *a* character of peculiar inadaptability to circumstances. Few people could have got on with him, and, as a matter of fact, he scarcely had an intimate friend throughout his life. The least suggestion of derogation from the most extravagant of his personal claims sufficed, especially in his later years, to inspire him with the keenest resentment. Schopenhauer was, in short, as perfect a type as we could well have of the completely self-centred egoist. Not that he lacked genuine zeal for truth, or devotion to philosophy. But these things were inseparable with him from zeal for the applause and recognition of his own work, and devotion to his own personality as such. That

Schopenhauer was not destitute of a certain sense of humour his writings show. But certainly there was something lacking in his feeling for the ridiculous, or otherwise he could never have penned the comically arrogant passages concerning himself which he has done. It is a susceptibility to the comic side of things which alone saves the man of greater ability than the average from the expression of exaggerated estimates of his own powers. (An excessive personal sensibility, leading at times to moroseness, an irritability of temper which exaggerated trifles, and a personal vanity of huge proportions, must, in short, be admitted as fundamental characteristics of the founder of the neo-pessimism. These things were associated with a timidity, a scenting of danger from afar, which, though it may have been, as it is with many, purely constitutional in its origin, yet was in his case unquestionably fostered and nourished by the excessive habit of self-concentration above alluded to. Schopenhauer was in a constant state of alarm as to his personal safety. He fled from the very name of an infectious disease. He was so afraid of fire that he would only live on the ground floor of the house; and his fear of reverse of fortune was so great that he was in the habit of concealing important business papers and other valuable property, lest it should be stolen, under the harmless label of "*materia medica.*" Still there can be no doubt whatever as to the sincerity of Schopenhauer's belief in his own mission, as the exponent of a new philosophy, or rather as the expounder in the definite formulae of Western thought of the old semi-poetical philosophy of the East.

THE PHILOSOPHY OF SCHOPENHAUER

By Ernest Belfort Bax

As he is never tired of insisting, Schopenhauer's philosophy is based upon the criticism of Kant. As already hinted, there were two distinct possibilities of speculative development contained in the Kantian metaphysic. Kant had divided his system into Transcendental Æsthetic, Transcendental Analytic, and Transcendental Dialectic. The first contained an exposition of the conditions of pure sensibility. These were for Kant the subsuming of the blind sense impression, the resultant of the unknown thing-in-itself uder the forms of space and time. But to the completed phenomenon of so-called common-sense reality — to the object known as such — another element was necessary, that, namely, of the pure activity of thought, working through certain categories tabulated by Kant, and deducible from the ultimate unity of the consciousness. The exposition of the pure thought-conditions — as opposed to those of pure sense — are set forth and discussed in the second part of the "Critique," which Kant terms "The Transcendental Analytic." These two first parts of the great work, since they deal, not with the completed reality as we find it, but with the conditions which that reality presupposes — with the elements which go to the making of that reality rather than with the reality as a whole — these two first parts of the "Critique" are called by Kant the "Theory of Elements" ("*elementarlehre*"). The remainder of the book consists in the so-called "Transcendental Dialectic." This no longer deals with the elements which go to the making or determination of reality in consciousness, but with the idea' or assumptions which the mind is compelled to super-impose on these, and which hinge on the conceptions of the soul as a simple substance, on the world infinite in time and space, and on God as the self-containing principle of all reality and all possibility of reality. The Sensibility, therefore, the faculty of receiving impressions from without; the Understanding, the faculty of working up these impressions into a coherent world of objects; and the Reason, the faculty of carrying on the process of thought-activity beyond the given world of phenomena created by the synthesis of sensibility and understanding, constitute for Kant the tripartite division of consciousness in general, or knowledge, in the widest sense of the word. Kant designated his system, therefore, as "Theory of Knowledge," inasmuch as it was an investigation into the conditions under which alone all knowledge is possible.

Now while Fichte, Schelling, and Hegel, especially the first and third, had taken their stand in the main upon the element of direct thought-activity deducible from the synthetic unity of the consciousness, and had thus postulated thought or intelligence as the ultimate principle of all reality, Schopenhauer thought he was able' to deduce the active, formative principle of the world from something still deeper, from a principle which was itself *a*logical, non-conscious — albeit the source of consciousness — a principle he identified with the so-called thing-in-itself, and the sense-impression which, according to Kant, was its result. This principle he further identified with Will, understanding by Will all *nisus,* all impulse, of whatever character. (The intelligence is, therefore, a secondary principle, entirely subordinate to the thing-in-itself, or Will, which manifests itself in all Nature, being substantially the same whether in gravitation or in human desire.' Will is for Schopenhauer the *matter,* the intelligence, the *form* of Reality, but the two elements are everywhere distinguishable in consciousness.' In Schopenhauer's first work, "The Fourfold Root," he had endeavoured to establish the proposition that all the Kantian categories are ultimately deducible from that of Cause, and that this is itself a mode of the Will. "Adequate Cause" is divided by Schopenhauer into a principle of being, doing, acting and knowing (*essendi, fiendi, agendi, and cognoscendi*). The law of Adequate Cause expresses the ordered connection between all our presentments, as determinable a *priori,* by virtue of which nothing can be self-existent and independent of other things, but in order to be an object for our consciousness it must stand in connection with the totality of phenomena. But the manner of this connection differs according to the nature of the object. Every presentment which can become object for us falls under one or other of four classes. The first class of possible objects of presentment is that of the completed empirical perception. The primary form of this perception Schopenhauer makes, following Kant, to consist in space and time, the forms respectively of the outer and of the inner sense. In this class of objects it appears as the law of causality in the narrower sense of the word. Schopenhauer calls it the law of the adequate cause of becoming (*principium rationis suflicientis fiend*). A change in any object or objects presupposes another, upon which it has followed, with absolute necessity. Such a sequence is what we commonly call cause and effect. The forms of causality in this sense are mechanical cause, organic irritability, and psychical motive. The first form, in which action and reaction are equal to one another, governs the inorganic world with its mechanical processes, the second governs the organic world with its physiological processes, and the third governs the world of thought and conscious action. The second class of possible objects for a subject are constituted by concepts or abstract presentments. This is the class concerned with the adequate cause of *knowing (principium rationis sufficientis cognoscendi)*, which proclaims that if a judgment is to express an intelligent proposition it must have a sufficient reason, hence it is termed true, truth consisting either in the logical and formal correctness of judgments, or in their adequacy for expressing a sensuous perception, which, in so far as it is based on experience, constitutes empirical truth. The third class of objects for the presentative faculty is constituted by the formal element of the completed presentments, namely, the a *priori* given intuitions of the forms of the external and the internal sense, *space* and *time.* As pure perceptions they are distinguishable from the completed objects of perception. They have the characteristic that all their parts stand in one relation to each other, in respect of which each of them is conditioned by the other. In space, this relation is called position; in time, sequence. From the latter *number* is directly deducible. The law according to which parts of time and space are determined is termed by Schopenhauer the law of the adequate cause of being *(principium rationis sufficientis essendi).* The fourth and last class of possible objects for the faculty of presentment has ifs basis in the immediate object of the internal sense, the subject which wills, but which is at the same time object for the faculty of presentment, though an object of a unique kind, being only given to the internal sense, and, therefore, manifesting itself, not in space, but in time alone. In respect of Willing, the law of cause presents itself as the law of sufficient reason of action, or as the law of motivation *(principium rations sufcientis agendi).* In so far as motive is the external condition of an action it belongs to causes of the same kind as those mechanical ones considered under the first class of objects of possible presentment. In this last class, therefore, the circle is complete, since in it the first class merely evinces itself as ultimately the same thing viewed from the external side only. For motives are known to us not only from without like other causes, but also from within, and in them, therefore, we have the key to the mystery of the innermost meaning of all other kinds of causation. Motivation is simply causation seen from within. Such is, in brief outline, the subject-matter of Schopenhauer's first philosophical work. Those desirous of further information respecting it may consult the English translation, which forms one of the volumes in Bohn's Philosophical Library.

Schopenhauer's "chief work," "The World as Will and Presentment," is divided into four sections, of which the first treats of The World as Presentment, in the sense of empirical reality, the object of science; the second, of The World as Will, that is, the will-to-live; the third, of The World as Presentment, so to say in its second intention, as Platonic Idea, the object of art; the fourth, lastly, of The Will in it., second intention, as purified from the lust of life, and turned as it were against itself. The volume ends with an appendix on the Kantian philosophy.

"The World is my Presentment." This proposition, with which the first book begins, applies, says Schopenhauer, to every living and knowing being, albeit in man alone does it appear in the form of a reflective or abstract thought. The sundering of consciousness into object and subject is the only form under which any presentment, be it perceptive or conceptive, is possible or thinkable. The world means simply the totality of objects existing in and for a subject, of perceptions for a perceiver, in short, of presentments; the whole world and all that can possibly belong to it is subject to this condition; it is only *there* for a subject, it is only a determination of a subject. The essential and universal forms of the object belong, however, to the subject, as Schopenhauer with Kant insists, and may, therefore, be distinguished a priori in consciousness. The principle of adequate cause, as expounded by Schopenhauer in the book above noticed, and at less length here, is the general expression which embraces all forms of the object. Materialism errs, in that it ignores the fact in question. The only valid standpoint consists in the recognition of the complete relativity involved in all presentment and in all thought. From this complete relativity, amounting with Schopenhauer to a dualism, Schopenhauer infers the *prius,* or root-principle, to be something other than intelligence or knowledge. The separation of subject and object, and the law of cause which it implies, involves us in an antinomy or contradiction. For although metaphysically the existence of the world is dependent on its being known by living beings, yet, physically, these latter are themselves just as dependent on a chain of physical events, of causes and effects, into which they enter as a mere link. This antinomy finds its solution in the assumption that the World as Presentment, that is, as sundered into subject and object and subordinated to the principle of cause, is only its external side, and that its innermost being, its kernel, its root, in short, the "thing-in-itself" of Kant, is what we term, with reference to its most direct and immediate manifestation, *Will.*

The second book treats of the objectivation of the *Will.* The body is presented in a double manner to the subject of knowledge, first as a mediate presentment, or object among other objects, and subordinated to the law of causation, and secondly as that immediately known to each. The act of the will and the movement of my body are not two different conditions standing in the relation to each other of cause and effect, but they are simply the same thing viewed from a double side. The action of the body is simply the act of will objectified. The question as to whether the remaining phenomena of the world, as known from the external side only, are acts of will or not, is really identical with the question as to whether they are reality or illusion.

To answer it in the negative amounts to a solipsism. This is indeed a sceptical sophism which cannot be refuted, but, on the other hand, it is a theory which no one holds outside a mad-house. Hence we are perfectly justified in assuming that the phenomenon manifested in the being or action of our own body is a key to that of all other phenomena in nature, although *they* are only given in presentment from the outer side. This means, that could we strip off their character of presentments in an intelligence, of objects for a consciousness, what remained over would be identical with that which in the case of our body we term Will. The Will considered as thing-in-itself is entirely distinct from the same Will as phenomenalized, objectivized, or presented in consciousness, and is not subject to the conditions of the latter, which conditions merely touch its objectivity. 'The will considered as thing-in-itself is one and indivisible, though its objective manifestations in the phenomenal world are infinite.' But these infinite manifestations, in so far as they are double-sided like our own organism, and therefore real, are of a mixed nature, and hence do not express the element of objectivity or outwardness in its purity. The latter is only to be found in the pure idea, which is at the root of every class of phenomena, that is, in the system of Ideal types, which constitute the successive stages in the objectivation of the Will, as more or less confusedly reproduced in the particular phenomena in which they express themselves. The most general forces of matter, such as gravity, impenetrability, &c., represent the lowest phase of the objectivation of the Will. Physical, chemical, and organic forces supervene on these, represent successively higher stages in the objectivation. Each stage contests its place in space and time with the one below it This applies not only to the more important stages; but also to the subordinate ones; for example, every higher form of life has to battle for its place in nature with those below it. As a consequence, it only expresses so much of the Mea as it has the force left in it to do after this conflict has been decided in its favour. Time and space as the *principia individiationis* have no immediate influence on the ideas, which as *pure objects* stand over and above the particulars or individuals in time and space which more or less adequately, more or less inadequately, embody them.

This doctrine is the basis of Schopenhauer's "theory of art," and is set forth in the third book of "The World as Will and Presentment." As we have seen, at one pole is the Will as pure Subject; at the other is the Presentment as pure Object. Between these two positions — these two modes of the *noumenon* or thing-in-itself — lies the phenomenal world, with its participation in both, under the conditions of Time, Space, and Causation in its four forms. The idea (the Platonic Idea, as Schopenhauer sometimes calls it), notwithstanding that it is not subject to the conditions of time and space, and the categories of cause, is nevertheless a form of knowledge — indeed, the most universal form of knowledge — it is *Presentment in general.* We can only attain through individual things to a knowledge of the ideas they represent, in so far as a change takes place in us — *i.e.,* in the percipient or subject of knowledge itself, by which the latter, in so far as it is absorbed in the apprehension of the idea, ceases, *pro hac vice,* to be individual, and becomes universal. This form of knowledge belongs exclusively to the objectivation of the will in its higher stages. In the first instance, the intellect, or faculty of knowledge, is entirely there in the service of the Will. But as the faculty of apprehending the idea it is emancipated from this service, the pleasure experienced in aesthetic contemplation being, Schopenhauer contends, will-less in its origin and nature. The capacity for abstracting the intellect from the service of the Will is the exclusive appanage of Man. With the animals the intellect always remains the slave of the appetites — that is, under the complete sway of the Will-to-live. Hence they are incapable of aesthetic contemplation. For the art-consciousness demands that we should regard the Object presented apart from its *why,* its *wherefore,* its *how,* and its *when.* In doing so, we approach the pure Platonic idea — the ideal type of the Object considered in itself. The Subject for the nonce is emancipated from its ordinary desires and impulses, apprehensions and interests, and becomes, so to speak, raised to a higher potency of consciousness. It is conscious no longer of the individual thing, but of the eternal form.

The different branches of the fine arts represent the different stages in the objectivation of the Will. The lowest stage is that of architecture, which embodies the idea of gravity, and the forces deducible from it — in short, it expresses the Platonic idea of what appears in the phenomenal world as mechanics. As we rise in the scale, the natural forces expressed become more complex, and the idea conveys with deeper meaning and greater precision the truth of human life. For example, painting, which deals directly with individuals or particulars, treats them only as the representatives of a class. They are for the artist not individuals, but types. The highest achievements of painting are to be found in mediaeval catholic art, which portrays the figure of the saint in whom the Will-to-live has died, and who has therefore already attained to a foretaste of Nirvana. The same with poetry: the highest manifestation of the poetic art is in tragedy.

Music stands on a different footing from the other arts, inasmuch as it does not represent any one stage of the Will's manifestation like them, but is the direct embodiment of the Will's objectivity in general. Hence the peculiar effect, unlike that of the other arts, which music produces on minds susceptible to it. In music we have the purest expression of the free play of emotion and impulse, undetermined to any specific subject-matter. Schopenhauer carries this idea out with much ingenuity as regards both harmony and melody, the different registers, cadences, rhythms, etc. Joy and sorrow, pure and simple, is, in short, the burden of music. There is no material, as in the other arts, which covers this central fact up, overloading it with detail which obscures the real issue, but all is here directly and obviously reducible to the blind impulse which Schopenhauer terms "The Will-to-live."

The fourth and last book of the "World as Will and Presentment" treats of the Will-to-live as turning against itself, as recognizing its own futility and denying itself. This can only be attained by means of the insight that all life issues in sorrow and pain; that the evil of the world outbalances the good, and does so not accidentally but necessarily. All Willing, Schopenhauer is fond of pointing out, implies want, and all want implies suffering: Hence so long as the Will is affirmed so long are evil and suffering affirmed. The root of all life being Willing, and all Willing implying the want of something which is not, as soon as one want is satisfied another arising by the very necessities of the case, it follows that the Will in us must be destroyed annihilated, before the blessed state of the extinction of all Willing, and of the consciousness, which is in the service of the Will, can be attained. A partial and temporary satisfaction may be acquired by the transformation of the Will into pure objectivity, as in the art-consciousness. But this is not enduring. We cannot continue in this state for long, we are continually forced back into that world in which the intellect, the intelligence, is in the service of the Will.

Hence the final solution of the problem of life is to be found, not in aesthetics, but in ethics; it is to be found, in short, in asceticisme. The destruction of the individual life is one thing, that of the Will-to-live is another. In the first it is the phenomenon only which perishes, leaving the *noumenon*, the thing-in-itself, or Will, remaining intact, and continuing to realize itself immediately in another individual. For this reason suicide is no solution of the difficulty, for the Will is affirmed in the very act by which the life is destroyed.

On the other hand, once the Will is finally negated, the continuance of the mere phenomenal life for a time is quite a secondary matter. The consequence of this, namely, self-starvation, the absention, as in the case of the Hindoo yogis, from all action on one's own behalf tending to preserve life as being the highest expression of an ascetic morality, is obvious, and Schopenhauer does not shrink from it. The great turning point in the negation of the Will-to-live is the triumph over the sexual impulse, the impulse which directly leads to the affirmation of the Will in new individuals. The final stage is the triumph over the Will-to-live as expressed in the instinct of self-preservation, that is, in the desire for the continuance of the immediate personality concerned. The Hindoo ascetics above all, and after them the Trappists, are Schopenhauer's ideal. The end of Schopenhauer's philosophy is the complete extinction of Will, and, as a natural consequence, of life itself, in all human beings, which is, therefore, the ultimate goal of all existence. The Will perishes, and the root of consciousness being cut away, it withers and dies. The blessed state of consciousless, Will-less extinction, the great Nothing which all Nature points, is then attained. Schopenhauer speaks of "the dark impression of that Nothing, which looms as the final goal behind all virtue and holiness, which we fear like children the darkness." "Instead of seeking to evade it," he concludes, "as even the Indians do by myths and meaningless words, or the Nirvana of the Buddhists, we recognize the fact freely that what remains after the complete abolition of the Will is for all those who are immersed in the Will assuredly nothing. But conversely, for those in whom the Will has turned against and denied itself, this our so very real world, with all its suns and galaxies, is also — nothing."

The above is a brief, and therefore necessarily extremely condensed, exposition of the leading principles of Schopenhauer's philosophy. Its merits and its defects are not far to seek for the philosophical student. Many, and sometimes deep, are the insights which we come across in all Schopenhauer's writings. The ingenuity with which he fits his own acute observations on men and things, on Nature and art, into his system, is sometimes quite startling. This is especially noticeable in the third book of "The World as Will and Presentment," which contains his theory of art. It is, in fact, on the artistic side that Schopenhauer has most directly influenced the world. His power in determining the theories of Richard Wagner, and thus indirectly in revolutionizing modern dramatic music, are well known, although it is curious to note that Schopenhauer himself did not appreciate the earlier works of Wagner, which were the only ones with which he was acquainted.

The ethical side of Schopenhauer's system has mainly served as a quasi-philosophical stalking-horse for the somewhat nebulous *fin de siècle* pessimism which is the characteristic note of the modern "man of culture." It has been expanded and developed by many a *littérateur*-philosopher, its most systematic latter-day exponent being Eduard Von Hartmann. Schopenhauer's purely literary merits as a writer of German are so great, that his books have penetrated into circles where no other philosophical literature obtains access. He has remained what he was when he first began to be read, the popularizer of philosophy for the general reading public. His theory is comparatively easy of apprehension by the man of average general education, who is not altogether destitute of speculative faculty or cravings, but who does not want the trouble of the arduous and sustained labour necessary to the thinking out of the metaphysical problem in all its bearings, or to the adequate comprehension of a thinker like Hegel. Schopenhauer's boasted clearness, on the other hand, is often the mere clearness of superficiality. As it has been justly observed, a mere specious illustration often serves the purpose of an argument. It is a similar superficiality, wearing the appearance of depth and knowledge of life, and taking its cue from the plausible but limited generalizations respecting what is known as "human nature" derived from observations of motives of men in the present day, and during the short span of time we term history, which is responsible for the cynicism so fashionable nowadays with the man of the world. To the latter any other attitude than that of cynicism and disbelief in "human nature" is evidence of mere infatuation, enthusiasm, or some other amiable weakness. Your man of the world is just as little able to entertain the suspicion that his cynicism is merely a passing mood, having its origin in himself, and in the particular phase of society which has given him birth, as the ancients were to conceive the possibility of the antipodes. To such an attitude of mind the pessimism of Schopenhauer is satisfactory, as supplying it with a quasi-philosophical justification. The denial of all progress and of any coherent development in human affairs, the natural consequence of the postulation of the individual as his own final *telos,* and the assertion in the most accentuated form of the introspective ethics, which has throughout history been the idealogical accompaniment of individualism in material things, all this is eminently congenial to the modern " cultured" man of the world.

In metaphysics Schopenhauer represents an

important, and, as far as it goes, a well-grounded protest against one tendency of the contemporary philosophy of his time, and especially of Hegel — the tendency, namely, to hypostatize the mere thought-form or category. Kant, in his deduction of the conditions under which all knowledge is possible, had started from the primitive "unity of apperception," as he termed it, as expressed in the self-conscious act, "I think." This, which with Kant was merely one side of a somewhat loosely connected theory, became with Fichte and with Hegel the keystone of the whole. While with Kant it had remained formal, with his successors it had become material as well — the root-principle of the Concrete or Real. In the "I think," stress was laid with them; as with Kant, on the "think." This is most noticeable in Hegel, where the "I" is a mere determination of the Concept, *i.e.*, of thinking. Now Schopenhauer caught at this one-sidedness, as it appeared to him, of the academic philosophy, and stoutly affirmed the principle that thought, or the logical, the "intelligible" principle in the constitution of reality, presupposed and was dependent on an *a*logical principle, which was identical with the thing-in-itself of Kant, which Hegel had eliminated from his system; that this was further identical with the Subject or "I" from which concepts and the consciousness they bring with them proceed — with the "I" which "thinks" — and that this "I" itself was merely another name for what under its most generalized aspect we term Will.

The above is really the special significance of Schopenhauer's system from a purely metaphysical standpoint. His opposition to the principle with which Hegel started, combined with the general bent of his mind, induced Schopenhauer to reject the greatest of all results of the German classical philosophy — a result to be found in germ in Kant, which was carried a step further by Fichte, and was perfected by Hegel — namely, the dialectical method. He was deeply impressed with the advantages of induction, which he believed could be applied to philosophy. This he had taken on as a part of his reaction against German thought, and of his prepossession in favour of the English empirical school. For him, therefore, the method which traces the unfolding of reality through contradiction and its resolution, was nothing but sophistry and a juggle of words, designed with the object of throwing dust in the eyes of the German learned public. Schopenhauer's quasi-inductive method of supporting his main thesis gave him the opportunity of bidding for popular applause by that introduction of illustration and plausible analogy, which has already been alluded to. The severe logical analysis of the academic thinkers was altogether repugnant to Schopenhauer's turn of mind. When he believed he had hit upon a deep metaphysical truth, he cast about him for facts in Nature which he might use in support of it. As a consequence, to the philosophical student trained on another method, the continued reiteration of the one fundamental proposition, all things are Will, in a form but little varied in itself, and merely reinforced from various sides, is somewhat wearisome, and is sometimes suggestive of Thales and his well-worn dictum, "all things are water."

At the same time, one cannot deny to Schopenhauer a certain genuine impartiality in the pursuit of truth. This is proved by the fact that his independent thought sometimes leads unconsciously to conclusions in flagrant opposition to his own sentiments and antipathies. Take for instance his utterances respecting the existing social system to be found in odd corners of his essays, or his arguments against "prescription" in vol. I., page 380, of "The World as Will and Presentment," and remember the bitterly reactionary sentiments of Schopenhauer in social and political matters generally. Mood is also a powerful factor in influencing Schopenhauer's utterances on various subjects of practical interest. He can sometimes work himself up into a state of vehement indignation, as when referring to English pietism and American negro slavery.

Notwithstanding the metaphysical truth enshrined in Schopenhauer's rehabilitation of the alogical element in knowledge — experience, or reality — as against the panlogism of Hegel and the academical school, and notwithstanding the wonderful suggestiveness of many portions of his work, especially his theory of art, it will be soon apparent to the attentive student that the coherence of the system, as a system, is very superficial. There is a good deal of unexplained residuum in it. Schopenhauer never seems quite clear as to the distinction between *abstract* and *concrete,* between *element* and *whole* or *thing.* For this reason, notwithstanding his protestations of Monism, his system really seems like a Dualism. According to his statement, the Will as thing-in-itself would seem to be not merely a basal element, but itself a *concrete,* a *thing* in the literal sense of the word. On the other hand, Presentment *as* Presentment seems to have likewise an independent existence. Thus, in the Platonic idea, the object of art, it exists apart from the Will, inasmuch as the element of Willing, as such, disappears, which would seem to contradict the assumption that the essence of the thing-in-itself is Will. Then, again, Schopenhauer never really gets over the difficulty involved in his ethical doctrine, according to which the Will-to-live can turn against and negate itself. This implies, look at it as we may, on Schopenhauer's principles, the destruction of a substance. The objection Schopenhauer himself was not unaware of, and in dealing with it he practically admits *willing* to be the mere attribute of a substratum in itself unknowable. Yet, again, the individualism of Schopenhauer's ethics involves some further difficulties. The one Will which is the soul of all things is in itself indivisible merely as object or phenomenon, as realizing itself in the conscious individual, under the forms of space, time, and causation, that the element of number enters into it. If this be true it cuts away the root of Schopenhauer's introspective-individualist ethics. For it is either wholly present in each individual or not. In either case the negation of the Will-to-live within him, as conscious and deliberate act on the part of any one individual *as* individual, cannot possibly affect the *noumenon* or thing-in-itself, which is identical in all individuals. To admit that it could do so would be to admit that very solipsism, that denial of reality as expressed in Willing to external things, against which Schopenhauer protests when discussing his theory of knowledge. No act of the phenomenal, conscious individual, on the principles of Schopenhauer's metaphysics, can in the least affect the root-principle of the Will which *ex hypothesi* manifests itself equally in all individuals. So long as one is left who dies unconverted, that is, without having of definite purpose renounced the Will-to-live, all things main as they were before, since there can in this sense be no question of degree as to the affirmation or denial of the Will. Either it is all there, or it is completely and absolutely abolished. Whether it survives and is affirmed in the consciousness of one individual or of a thousand trillions of individuals, cannot make the slightest difference in the case of that for which plurality in the last resort has no meaning. The only way out of this difficulty for Schopenhauer, and that a not very successful one it must be admitted, would have been to have postulated the act of renunciation as performed once for all by the deliberate and unanimous consent of all conscious beings, and to have held this out as the goal of history. But to have done so would have been to surrender the individualism which covers Schopenhauer's whole ethical theory, and to have got again into line, albeit in an opposite direction, with the notion of human evolution and historical progress, and for this the individualism of Schopenhauer's temperament was too strong.

As regards the whole question of Pessimism *versus* Optimism, it is extremely difficult for the man of today to realize that the problem involves an antinomy, and is therefore unanswerable, simply because it is wrongly stated. The problem is stated in terms of individual feeling as measured by quantity, while its subject-matter really transcends individual feeling, and is incommensurable. It is asked, Does the amount of pleasure experienced by the organic individual — an average individual being assumed — exceed, on the whole, the sum of pain experienced by the same individual or not? It is further asked with reference to the said individual, Does this in the natural course of things tend to become greater or less? The question then arises as to quality, expressed in the well-known conundrum whether the pig happy would be preferable to Socrates miserable. In all these ways of putting the problem, it is the organic individual, the present conscious unit, (and his immediate pleasures or pains,) which is alone taken into consideration. Looked at in this way the question is answered by different persons differently, according to character, circumstance, mood, etc., and each, whichever side he takes up, can find support in plausible illustrations. An array of facts can be adduced in favour of the one side or of the other. In all this, however, the real gist of the question is more often than not missed. All the time, moreover, the assumption is made that the organic individual is the self-sufficient and final arbiter in the matter. Viewed from this point of view it cannot be denied that pessimists have the best of it as a general rule, but their assumption, like that of the consistent sceptic as to the reality of the external world — that solipsist who so often reappears in the history of philosophy — is given the lie to by the facts of existence, notwithstanding plausible, and from one point of view unanswerable, theoretical arguments. The average conscious being *does* prefer existence to non-existence. This is a fact which remains to be explained. The philosophical pessimist, like Schopenhauer, explains it on the theory of illusion. The illusion has first to be pierced and seen through by the intellectual insight before emancipation from the illusion is possible. The answer to Schopenhauer as regards such an explanation might be, that when it is seen through intellectually the illusion is clung to notwithstanding. Schopenhauer himself is a case in point, for judged of from his purely individualistic point of view it is no mere *argumentum ad hominem* to taunt him with his own character and life as a disproof of his theory. It would surely not be unfair to assume that the man who, on his own showing, had more than any other man in Western Europe, by dint of intellectual insight, seen through the delusion as to the worth of life, and recognized self-destruction through ascetic privation as its highest end, ought to have practically realized his doctrine in his own person. That precisely he of all men had perhaps more than usual regard for the preservation of his own life under conditions of the greatest material comfort he could obtain, while those who have followed out the ascetic ideal to its practical consequences have been in many cases, perhaps in most cases, ignorant persons, actuated avowedly only by superstitious motives, certainly does not lend any colour or support to the theory on which Schopenhauer insists, to wit, that intellectual conviction of their futility tends to lead men to the renunciation of the pleasures of life, and ultimately life itself.

May not the strength of the practical conviction that life is worth living, in defiance of all theoretical proofs that it is not, afford evidence of the inaccuracy of Schopenhauer's assumption that pain is positive and pleasure negative, and also some confirmation of the fact that the significance of the individual is not exhausted within the limits of his own personality? This latter point is brought out more particularly by a consideration of the question of *quality* in pleasure or happiness. From the standpoint of pure Hedonism, that is, of a theory which merely balances pleasures and pains quantitatively, there can be no doubt whatever the choice must be in favour of being a contented swine rather than a discontented genius. Similarly *à fortiori* it must be quite plain that the greatest sum of animal enjoyment conceivable for the healthy man may possibly, nay, will probably, be greater in amount for the individual who experiences it than the highest amount of pleasure to be derived by the man of correspondingly vigorous intellectual powers and refined tastes from intellectual things. But yet we have an unshakable conviction, the reverse of which is, in fact, taken seriously, unthinkable, that there is something preferable in the one to the other; that the difference of quality upsets all calculations based on mere quantity — in other words, that the question of mere pleasure and pain, taken in the abstract and referred to the individual also regarded abstractly, simply involves us in a circle from which there is no escape, but which does not get us any further forward in the solution of the problem of human life taken in the concrete. Mere pleasure or happiness, considered abstractly, may for practical purposes be regarded as a proximate end, and, in a similar way, the individual considered in himself, and apart from the social life and progress into which he enters, may also for practical purposes be regarded as a proximate end to himself. But we must never forget that so long as we regard things in this way we are dealing with abstractions which appear very differently when viewed from the standpoint of the meaning of the world and human nature considered as a real synthesis. In proportion as this proximate aim assumes the form for us of a supreme end, we are living on a lower plane, since we are unmindful of the point of view from which the individual personality becomes a mere component or element of a larger whole. This position is most fully seen in the personality which we describe as criminal, or immoral in the true sense of the word, that is, anti-social. But it is also characteristic in a lesser degree of the commonplace man of the world. The aim of the introspective morality, the morality, that is, whose sign-manual throughout history is the ideal of personal holiness, as attained through the mere negation of the individual, his impulses and desires, has been to change this *per saltum* by means of asceticism. But in asceticism the egoistic point of view is not really abandoned, but is merely inverted. Self-denial for self-denial's sake belongs intrinsically just as much to the egoistic attitude as the mere self-indulgence of the libertine. In both cases the individual is viewed as end, that is, he is considered abstractly. The really higher point of view which transcends both these attitudes alike, is that which recognizes the personality and its immediate pleasure and pain as indeed constituting a proximate or immediate end, that is, a necessary stage, which, though not ultimate, is none the less an essential element in any higher end to which we may aspire; and which further recognizes that the only lasting and effective manner in which what we may term the *abstract* egoistic instincts can be abolished is in the identification by the sheer necessity of circumstances of individual pleasure and pain — in short, individual interest, in the narrower sense, with the interest of the whole of human society. The lower or anti-social impulses, then, so to speak, abolish themselves. To borrow Schopenhauer's phraseology, the affirmation of the Will-to-live in the individual becomes absorbed in, and identical with, the affirmation of the Will-to-live of humanity as a whole. The strain of antagonism between the two, which from the lower standpoint seemed absolute, disappears. This is a stage, however, at which the ethical and economical problems intersect. I merely refer to it here as indicating the fallacy of estimating pleasure and pain, happiness and unhappiness, in terms of quantity merely, and with exclusive reference to the individual. Whether the abolition by the transformation of social conditions of the antagonism at present existing between individual and social interest is the prelude to a cycle of evolution, the end of which will be the transference of the characteristics of personality from the organic individual to the social individual (as we may term it), understanding by this a given society in its collective capacity, is a question which, extravagant and even incomprehensible though it may seem to many, nevertheless forces itself irresistibly upon one in reflecting on the problem as to the meaning of human life as we know it, and which opens up a vista of unknown possibilities, before which arguments drawn from our own limited data shrink into nothing.

On the question as to the tendency of progress towards an increase of happiness or the reverse, many reflections may be and have been made. The observation of the limited period passed through between the younger world and today, seems to indicate rather a change in the distribution of the relative happiness and misery of the world than any increase or diminution of either. The ease seems to be expressed by such a fact as this, for example: the hardships of the mediaeval serf, the acute and devastating epidemics of the Middle Ages, the ever-present possibilities of fire and sword, the torture-chambers of the feudal castle and of the inquisition, the recurrent famines continually imminent in one locality or another — all these things have been mitigated, and some have passed away altogether. But they have been replaced by the ever-present mass of misery of the present day, as represented by the proletariat of our large towns, and by all that our modern polarization of the extremes of wealth and poverty implies. Similarly, the naïve exuberance of animal spirits and un: restrained enjoyment of the Middle Ages, work-days and holidays alike, has vanished, and its place has been taken by the subdued bourgeois equanimity of the suburban villa, or the vapid inanities of the London season and its drawing-rooms. Still, all this affords us no valid grounds for the induction as regards future change, the conditions of which must necessarily be entirely different.

The fact is, the antithesis between what in its most comprehensive aspect we designate by the words *good* and *evil* must continue in some form or shape, since they are elements mutually implicated in every *Real.* As to the increase or decrease of the one relatively to the other, we can only judge indirectly; the state of the case being, that all specific, that is, realized evil, necessarily passes away — that what is permanent is merely, so to say, the abstract category, *evil-in-general* undetermined to any specific content. But although at first sight the same is true of the opposite, namely, of the *good*, yet the case is not precisely identical, for while the preponderance of the specific or concrcte evil to be eliminated appears at the beginning of a cycle of progress, or of a specific dialectical movement of evolution, the preponderance of "the good" attained through its elimination, as expressed in the *reality* of the cycle in question, invariably appears as the end and completion of that cycle. This implies, as will be readily seen, a "point" in the evolutionary process, as always given in favour of the "good." It implies, that is, that the trend of progress is towards the "good," though the approximation may be entirely of an asymptotic character. A reflection of this kind may indeed destroy extravagant optimism, and cause the youthful enthusiasm of those who are satisfied with nothing less than a perfection, which, when closely viewed, is simply meaningless, because abstract, and hence in its nature unrealizable, to be "sicklied o'er with the pale cast of thought." Yet for the more sober-minded enthusiast it is none the less a consolation the more valuable as resting on a philosophical truth which cannot be taken away from him, to feel that the end of every evolutionary cycle implies an increase of happiness as against its beginning. This good, or happiness, it is true — this victory of Ormuzd over Arhiman — is not enduring, inasmuch as its very conditions contain the *nidus* of a further and distinct evil of its own, unknown before, and which sooner or later makes its presence evident. But, nevertheless, in spite of this, the fact remains that in the moment of realization there is a positive and real increment of good or of happiness over the opposing principle. The old "evil" is destroyed, the new is as yet unrealized. To this process of the continual absorption of specific evil or misery in infinitely changing shape, by good or happiness, also in infinitely changing shape and on a progressively higher level, we can assign no end.

The foregoing are considerations which Schopenhauer might have seen but did not, and which, if he had seen, would certainly have modified his philosophico-ethical conclusions.

THE METAPHYSICS OF THE SEXUAL LOVE

From Schopenhauer, "The world as will and idea", vol. II. *Geschlechtsliebe* corresponds to "sexual love", in relation to the distinction between the sexes and to the generation.

"Ye wise men, highly, deeply learned,
Who think it out and know,
How, when, and where do all things pair?
Why do they kiss and love?
Ye men of lofty wisdom, say
What happened to me then;
Search out and tell me where, how, when,
And why it happened thus." — Bürger

This chapter[1] is the last of four whose various reciprocal relations, by virtue of which, to a certain extent, they constitute a subordinate whole, the attentive reader will recognize without it being needful for me to interrupt my exposition by recalling them or referring to them.

We are accustomed to see poets principally occupied with describing the love of the sexes. This is as a rule the chief theme of all dramatic works, tragical as well as

---

[1] The chapters XLI (On Death) and XLIV (The Metaphysics of Sexual Love) govern chapter XLII (Life of the Species) and chapter XLIII (« The Hereditary Nature of Qualities».)

comical, romantic as well as classical, Indian as well as European. Not less is it the material of by far the largest part of lyrical and also of epic poetry, especially if we class with the latter the enormous piles of romances which for centuries every year has produced in all the civilised countries of Europe as regularly as fruits of the earth[2]. As regards their main contents, all these works are nothing else than many-sided brief or lengthy descriptions of the passion we are speaking of. Moreover, the most successful pictures of it — such, for example, as *Romeo and Juliet*, *La Nouvelle Heloise*, and *Werther* — have gained immortal fame. Yet, when Rochefoucauld imagines that it is the same with passionate love as with ghosts, of which ever one speaks, but which no one has seen; and Lichtenberg also in his essay, "On the power of love (*Ueber die Macht der Liebe*)," disputes and denies the reality and naturalness of that passion, they are greatly in error. For it is impossible that something which is foreign and contrary to human nature, thus a mere imaginary caricature, could be unweariedly represented by poetic genius in all ages, and received by mankind with unaltered interest; for nothing that is artistically beautiful can be without truth: —

---

[2] Note the biological image and the rapprochement between the novel and the epic.

"Rein n'est beau que le vrai; le vrai seul est amiable."
(Boileau)

Certainly, however, it is also confirmed by experience, although not by the experience of every day, that that which as a rule only appears as a strong yet still controllable inclination may rise under certain circumstances to a passion which exceeds all others in vehemence, and which then sets aside all considerations, overcomes all obstacles with incredible strength and perseverance, so that for its satisfaction life is risked without hesitation, nay, if that satisfaction is still withheld, is given as the price of it. Werthers and Jacopo Ortis exist not only in romance, but every year can show at least a half a dozen of them in Europe: "But those deaths were ignored. (*Sed ignotis perierunt mortibus illi*)"; for their sorrows find no other chroniclers than the writers of official registers or the reporters of the newspapers. Yet the readers of the police news in English and French journals will attest the correctness of my assertion. Still greater, however, is the number of those whom the same passion brings to the madhouse. Finally, every year can show cases of the double suicide of a pair of lovers who are opposed by outward circumstances. In such cases, however, it is inexplicable to me how those who, certain of mutual love, expect to find the supreme bliss in the enjoyment of this, do not withdraw themselves from all connections by taking the extreme steps, and endure all hardships, rather than give up with life a pleasure which is greater than any other they can conceive. As regards the lower grades of that passion, and the mere approaches to it, every one has them daily before his eyes, and, as long as he is not old, for the most part also in his heart.

So then, after what has been called to mind, no one can doubt either the reality or the importance of the matter; and therefore, instead of wondering that a philosophy should also for once make its own this constant theme of all poets, one ought rather to be surprised that a thing which plays throughout so important a part in human life has hitherto practically been disregarded by philosophers altogether, and lies before us as raw material. The one who has most concerned himself with it is Plato, especially in the "Symposium" and the "Phaedrus". Yet what he says on the subject is confined to the sphere of myths, fables, and jokes, and also for the most part concerns only the Greek love of youths. The little that Rousseau says upon our theme in the "*Discours sur l'inegalité*"[3] (p. 96,

---

[3] In 1754, Rousseau presented this speech at the contest of the

ed. Bip.) is false and insufficient. Kant's explanation of the subject in the third part of the essay, "*Observations on the Feeling of the Beautiful and Sublime* (*Beobachtungen über das Gefühl des Schönen und Erhabenen)*" (p. 435 *seq.* of Rosenkranz' edition) is very superficial and without practical knowledge, therefore it is also partly incorrect. Lastly, Platner's treatment of the matter in his "Anthropology" (*sect.* 1347 *seq.*) every one will find dull and shallow. On the other hand, Spinoza's definition, on account of its excessive naivety, deserves to be quoted for the sake of amusement: "Love is pleasure, accompanied by the idea of an external cause (*Amor est titillatio, concomitante idea causae externae)*" (*Eth.* iv., prop. 44, *dem.*). Accordingly I have no predecessors either to make use of or to refute. The subject has pressed itself upon me objectively, and has entered of its own accord into the connection of my consideration of the world. Moreover, least of all can I hope for approbation from those who are themselves under the power of this passion, and who accordingly seek to express the excess of their feelings in the sublimest and most ethereal images. To them my view will appear too physical, too material, however metaphysical and even transcendent it may be at bottom. Meanwhile let them reflect that if the object

Academy of Dijon.

which today inspires them to write madrigals and sonnets had been born eighteen years earlier it would scarcely have won a glance from them.

For all love, however ethereally it may bear itself, is rooted in the sexual impulse alone, nay, it absolutely is only a more definitely determined, specialised, and indeed in the strictest sense individualised sexual impulse. If now, keeping this in view, one considers the important part which the sexual impulse in all its degrees and nuances plays not only on the stage and in novels, but also in the real world, where, next to the love of life, it shows itself the strongest and most powerful of motives, constantly lays claim to half the powers and thoughts of the younger portion of mankind, is the ultimate goal of almost all human effort, exerts an adverse influence on the most important events, interrupts the most serious occupations every hour, sometimes embarrasses for a while even the greatest minds, does not hesitate to intrude with its trash interfering with the negotiations of statesmen and the investigations of men of learning, knows how to slip its love letters and locks of hair even into ministerial portfolios and philosophical manuscripts, and no less devises daily the most entangled and the worst actions, destroys the most valuable relationships, breaks the firmest bonds, demands the sacrifice sometimes of life or health, sometimes of wealth, rank, and happiness, nay, robs those who are otherwise honest of all conscience, makes those who have hitherto been faithful, traitors; accordingly, on the whole, appears as a malevolent demon that strives to pervert, confuse, and overthrow everything; — then one will be forced to cry, Wherefore all this noise? Wherefore the straining and storming, the anxiety and want? It is merely a question of every Hans finding his Grethe[4]. Why should such a trifle play so important a part, and constantly introduce disturbance and confusion into the well-regulated life of man? But to the earnest investigator the spirit of truth gradually reveals the answer. It is no trifle that is in question here; on the contrary, the importance of the matter is quite proportionate to the seriousness and ardour of the effort. The ultimate aim of all love affairs, whether they are played in sock or cothurnus, is really more important than all other ends of human life, and is therefore quite worthy of the profound seriousness with which everyone pursues it. That which is decided by it is nothing less than the *composition of the next generation*. The characters of the drama (*dramatis personae*[5]) who shall appear when we are withdrawn are

---

[4] Schopenhauer adds this note: "Here I did not dare to express in precise terms: the willing reader will translate the phrase in an Aristophanic language".

here determined, both as regards their existence and their nature, by these frivolous love affairs. As the being, the existence (*existentia*)[6], of these future persons is absolutely conditioned by our sexual impulse generally, so their nature, *essentia*, is determined by the individual selection in its satisfaction, *i.e.*, by sexual love, and is in every respect irrevocably fixed by this. This is the key of the problem: we shall arrive at a more accurate knowledge of it in its application if we go through the degrees of love, from the passing inclination to the vehement passion, when we shall also recognise that the difference of these grades arises from the degree of the individualisation of the choice.

---

[5] *Dramatis personae*, Latin phrase referring to the list of characters in a play.

[6] The distinction between being and existence corresponds to the in-itself and to the phenomenon. The existence is temporal: what exists appears and disappears, is born and dies in the spatial and temporal limits of representation. Being is in itself will, as it manifests itself in the diversity of the phenomenal world, in the multiplicity of existences of which it is somehow the "core", to paraphrase a frequent image in the text of Schopenhauer. Even in an expression like "living beings", there is reference to the will-to-live and the individual will is not least in its bottom will, that is to say, a being in itself. Despite the suggestion of Schopenhauer who often seeks to rediscover the traditional vocabulary, we cannot translate "Wesen", that is to say, the will as manifested in the individual, by "essence", which would designate the species.

The collective love affairs of the present generation taken together are accordingly, of the whole human race, the serious "meditation of the human race as a whole on the composition of generations to come, on which in turn countless generations depend (*meditatio compositionis generationis futurae, e qua iterum pendent innumerae generations*)". This high importance of the matter, in which it is not a question of individual weal or woe, but of the existence and special nature of the human race in future times, and therefore the will of the individual appears at a higher power as the will of the species; — this it is on which the pathetic and sublime elements in affairs of love depend, which for thousands of years poets have never wearied of representing in innumerable examples; because no theme can equal in interest this one, which stands to all others which only concern the welfare of individuals as the solid body to the surface, because it concerns the weal and woe of the species. Just on this account, then, it is so difficult to impart interest to a drama without the element of love, and, on the other hand, this theme is never worn out even by daily use.

That which presents itself in the individual consciousness as sexual impulse in general, without being directed towards a definite individual of the other sex, is in itself, and apart from the phenomenon, simply the will to live. But what appears in consciousness as a sexual impulse directed to a definite individual is in itself the will-to-live as a definitely determined individual. Now in this case the sexual impulse, although in itself a subjective need, knows how to assume very skilfully the mask of an objective admiration, and thus to deceive our consciousness; for nature requires this stratagem to attain its ends. But yet that in every case of falling in love, however objective and sublime this admiration may appear, what alone is looked to in the production of an individual of a definite nature is primarily confirmed by the fact that the essential matter is not the reciprocation of love, but possession, *i.e.*, the physical enjoyment. The certainty of the former can therefore by no means console us for the want of the latter; on the contrary, in such a situation many a man has shot himself. On the other hand, persons who are deeply in love, and can obtain no return of it, are contented with possession, *i.e.*, with the physical enjoyment. This is proved by all forced marriages, and also by the frequent purchase of the favour of a woman, in spite of her dislike, by large presents and other sacrifices, nay, even by cases of rape. That this particular child shall be begotten is, although unknown to the parties concerned, the true end of the whole love story; the manner in which it is attained is a secondary consideration. Now, however loudly persons of lofty and sentimental soul, and especially those who are in love, may cry out here about the gross realism of my view, they are yet in error. For is not the definite determination of the individualities of the next generation a much higher and more worthy end than those exuberant feelings and supersensible soap bubbles of theirs? Nay, among earthly aims, can there be one which is greater or more important? It alone corresponds to the profoundness with which passionate love is felt, to the seriousness with which it appears, and the importance which it attributes even to the trifling details of its sphere and occasion. Only so far as this end is assumed as the true one do the difficulties encountered, the infinite exertions and annoyances made and endured for the attainment of the loved object, appear proportionate to the matter. For it is the future generation, in its whole individual determinateness, that presses into existence by means of those efforts and toils. Nay, it is itself already active in that careful, definite and arbitrary choice for the satisfaction of the sexual impulse which we call love. The growing inclination of two lovers is really already the will-to-live of the new individual which they can and desire to produce; nay, even in the meeting of their longing glances its new life breaks out, and announces itself as a future individuality harmoniously and well composed. They feel the longing for an actual union and fusing together into a single being, in order to live on only as this; and this longing receives its fulfilment in the child which is produces by them, as that in which the qualities transmitted by them both, fused and united in one being, live on. Conversely, the mutual, decided, and persistent aversion between a man and a maid is a sign that what they could produce would only be a badly organised, in itself inharmonious and unhappy being. Hence there lies a deeper meaning in the fact that Calderon, though he calls the atrocious Semiramis (the daughter of the air), yet introduces her as the daughter of rape followed by the murder of the husband.[7]

But, finally, what draws two individuals of different sex exclusively to each other with such power is the will to live, which exhibits itself in the whole species, and which here anticipates in the individual which these two can produce an objectification of its nature according to its aims. This individual will have the will, or character[8], from the father, the intellect from the mother, and the

---

[7] "The daughter of the air", title of a play of Calderon (1600-1681), Spanish writer highly appreciated and often quoted by Schopenhauer.

[8] Character that determines the entire sequence of actions of the individual, even his consciously voluntary actions.

corporization from both; yet, for the most part, the figure will take more after the father, the size after the mother, — according to the law which comes out in the breeding of hybrids[9] among the brutes, and principally depends upon the fact that the size of the foetus must conform to the size of the uterus. Just as inexplicable as the quite special individuality of any man, which is exclusively peculiar to him, is also the quite special and individual passion of two lovers; indeed at bottom the two are one and the same: the former is *explicite* what the latter was *implicite*. The moment at which the parents begin to love each other — to fancy each other, as the very happy English expression has it — is really to be regarded as the first appearance of a new individual and the true "point of origin (*punctum saliens*)" of its life, and, as has been said, in the meeting and the fixing of their longing glances there appears the first germ of the new being, which certainly, like all germs, is generally crushed out. This new individual is to a certain extent a new (Platonic) Idea; and now, as all Ideas strive with the greatest vehemence to enter the phenomenal world, eagerly seizing for this end upon the matter which the law of causality divides among them

---

[9] Hybridization is the combination of different species, for example, the mule is the result of the combination between the ass and the mare. Schopenhauer's scientific idea is based on the state of the science of his time.

all, so also does this particular Idea of a human individuality strive with the greatest eagerness and vehemence towards its realisation in the phenomenon. This eagerness and vehemence is just the passion of the two future parents for each other. It has innumerable degrees, the two extremes of which may at any rate be described as *Aphrodite pandemos* and *ourania*[10]; in its nature, however, it is everywhere the same. On the other hand, it will be in degree so much the more powerful the more *individualised* it is; that is, the more the loved individual is exclusively suited; by virtue of all his or her parts and qualities, to satisfy the desire of the lover and the need established by his or her own individuality. What is really in question here will become clear in the further course of our exposition. Primarily and essentially the inclination of love is directed to health, strength, and beauty, consequently also to youth; because the will first of all seeks to exhibit the specific character of the human species as the basis of all individuality: ordinary amorousness (*Aphrodite*

[10] *Aphrodite pandemos*, the elder daughter of Zeus and of Diana, is to Homeric tradition, *Aphrodite ourania*, who was born by the foaming semen on the sea around shreds of the flesh of Uranus who was mutilated by his son Cronus, is to Hesiodic tradition. Daughter of Uranus who hasn't a mother, she is, in this sense, Uranian or celestial and is far older than the other and even all the inhabitants of Olympus. These two divinities had each their temple in Athens and their cult. Plato contrasts these two loves in the "Symposium".

pandemos) does not go much further. To these, then, more special claims link themselves on, which we will investigate in detail further on, and with which, when they see satisfaction before them, the passion increases. But the highest degrees of this passion spring from the suitableness of two individualities to each other on account of which the will, *i.e.*, the character of the father and the intellect of the mother, in their connection, make up precisely that individual towards which the will-to-live in general which exhibits itself in the whole species feels a longing proportionate to this; its magnitude, and which therefore exceeds the measure of a mortal heart, and the motives of which, in the same way, lie beyond the sphere of the individual intellect. This is thus the soul of a true and great passion. Now the more perfect is the mutual adaptation of two individuals to each other in each of the many respects which have further to be considered, the stronger will be their mutual passion. Since there do not exist two individuals exactly alike, there must be for each particular man a particular woman — always with reference to what is to be produced — who corresponds most perfectly. A really passionate love is as rare as the accident of these two meeting. Since, however, the possibility of such a love is present in everyone, the representations of it in the works of the poets are comprehensible to us. Just because the passion of love really turns about that which is to be produced, and its qualities, and because its kernel lies there, a friendship without any admixture of sexual love can exist between two young and good-looking persons of different sex, on account of the agreement of their disposition, character, and mental tendencies; nay, as regards sexual love there may even be a certain aversion between them. The reason of this is to be sought in the fact that a child produced by them would have physical or mental qualities which were inharmonious; in short, its existence and nature would not answer the ends of the will-to-live as it exhibits itself in the species. On the other hand, in the case of difference of disposition, character, and mental tendency, and the dislike, nay, enmity, proceeding from this, sexual love may yet arise and exist, when it then blinds us to all that; and if it here leads to marriage it will be a very unhappy one.

Let us now set about the more thorough investigation of the matter. Egoism is so deeply rooted a quality of all individuals in general, that in order to rouse the activity of an individual being egoistical ends are the only ones upon which we can count with certainty. Certainly the species has an earlier, closer, and greater claim upon the individual than the perishable individuality itself. Yet when the individual has to act, and even make sacrifices for the continuance and quality of the species, the importance of the matter cannot be made so comprehensible to the intellect, which is calculated merely with regard to individual ends, as to have its proportionate effect. Therefore in such a case nature can only attain its ends by implanting a certain illusion in the individual, on account of which that which is only a good for the species appears to him as a good for himself, so that when he serves the species he imagines he is serving himself; in which process a mere chimera, which vanishes immediately afterwards, floats before him, and takes the place of a real thing as a motive. This illusion is instinct. In the great majority of cases this is to be regarded as the sense of the species, which presents what is of benefit to it to the will. Since, however, the will has here become individual, it must be so deluded that it apprehends through the sense of the individual what the sense of the species presents to it, thus imagines it is following individual ends while in truth it is pursuing ends which are merely general (taking this word in its strictest sense). The external phenomenon of instinct we can best observe in the brutes where its role is most important; but it is in ourselves alone that we arrive at a knowledge of its internal process, as of everything internal. Now it is certainly supposed that man has almost no instinct; at any rate only this, that the new-born babe seeks for and seizes the breast of its mother. But, in fact, we have a very definite, distinct, and complicated instinct, that of the selection of another individual for the satisfaction of the sexual impulse, a selection which is so fine, so serious, and so arbitrary.[11] With this satisfaction in itself, *i.e.*, so far as it is a sensual pleasure resting upon a pressing want of the individual, the beauty or ugliness of the other individual has nothing to do. Thus the regard for this which is yet pursued with such ardor, together with the careful selection which springs from it, is evidently connected, not with the chooser himself — although he imagines it to be so — but with the true end, that which is to be produced, which is to receive the type of the species as purely and correctly as possible. Through a thousand physical accidents and moral aberrations there arise a great variety of deteriorations of the human form; yet its true type, in all its parts, is always again established: and this takes place under the guidance of the sense of beauty, which always directs the sexual impulse, and without which this sinks to the level of a disgusting necessity. Accordingly, in the first place, every one will decidedly prefer and eagerly desire the most beautiful

---

[11] By introducing the theme of individualized choice of love, Schopenhauer escapes from the reductive and usual alternative of the biological and the spiritual.

individuals, *i.e.*, those in whom the character of the species is most purely impressed; but, secondly, each one will specially regard as beautiful in another individual those perfections which he himself lacks, nay, even those imperfections which are the opposite of his own. Hence, for example, little men love big women, fair persons like dark, etc. The delusive ecstasy which seizes a man at the sight of a woman whose beauty is suited to him, and pictures to him a union with her as the highest good, is just the *sense of the species*, which, recognizing the distinctly expressed stamp of the same, desires to perpetuate it with this individual. Upon this decided inclination to beauty depends the maintenance of the type of the species: hence it acts with such great power. We shall examine specially further on the considerations which it follows. Thus what guides man is really an instinct which is directed to doing the best for the species, while the man himself imagines that he only seeks the heightening of his own pleasure. In fact, we have in this an instructive lesson concerning the inner nature of all instinct, which, as here, almost always sets the individual in motion for the good of the species. For clearly the pains with which an insect seeks out a particular flower, or fruit, or dung, or flesh, or as in the case of the *ichneumonidae*, the larva of another insect, in order to deposit its eggs there only, and to attain this end shrinks from neither trouble nor danger, is thoroughly analogous to the pains with which for his sexual satisfaction a man carefully chooses a woman with definite qualities which appeal to him individually, and strives so eagerly after her that in order to attain this end he often sacrifices his own happiness in life, contrary to all reason, by a foolish marriage, by love affairs which cost him wealth, honour, and life, even by crimes such as adultery or rape, all merely in order to serve the species in the most efficient way, although at the cost of the individual, in accordance with the will of nature which is everywhere sovereign. Instinct, in fact, is always an act which seems to be in accordance with the conception of an end, and yet is entirely without such a conception. Nature implants it wherever the acting individual is incapable of understanding the end, or would be unwilling to pursue it. Therefore, as a rule, it is given only to the brutes, and indeed especially to the lowest of them which have least understanding; but almost only in the case we are here considering it is also given to man, who certainly could understand the end, but would not pursue it with the necessary ardour, that is, even at the expense of his individual welfare. Thus here, as in the case of all instinct, the truth assumes the form of an illusion, in order to act upon the will. It is a voluptuous illusion which leads the man to believe he will find a greater pleasure in the arms of a woman whose beauty appeals to him than in those of any other; or which indeed, exclusively directed to a single individual, firmly convinces him that the possession of her will ensure him excessive happiness. Therefore he imagines he is taking trouble and making sacrifices for his own pleasure, while he does so merely for the maintenance of the regular type of the species, or else a quite special individuality, which can only come from these parents, is to attain an existence. The character of instinct is here so perfectly present, thus an action which seems to be in accordance with the conception of an end, and yet is entirely without such a conception, that he who is drawn by that illusion often abhors the end which alone guides it, procreation, and would like to hinder it; thus it is in the case of almost all illicit love affairs. In accordance with the character of the matter which has been explained, every lover will experience a marvellous disillusion after the pleasure he has at last attained, and will wonder that what was so longingly desired accomplishes nothing more than every other sexual satisfaction; so that he does not see himself much benefited by it. That wish was related to all his other wishes as the species is related to the individual, thus as the infinite to the finite. The satisfaction, on the other hand, is really only for the benefit of the species, and thus does not come within the consciousness of the individual, who, inspired by the will of the species, has served an end with every kind of sacrifice, which was not his own end at all. Hence, then, every lover, after the ultimate consummation of the great work, finds himself cheated; for the illusion has vanished by means of which the individual was here the dupe of the species. Plato very happily says, "Pleasure is the greatest of all vain talkers (*voluptas omnium maxime vaniloqua*)"(Plato, *Phileb*).

But all this reflects light on the instincts and mechanical tendencies of the brutes. They are also, without doubt, involved in a kind of illusion, which deceives them with the prospect of their own pleasure, while they work so laboriously and with such self-denial for the species, the bird builds his nest, the insect seeks the only suitable place for its eggs, or even hunts for prey which, unsuited for its own enjoyment, must be laid beside the eggs as food for the future larvae, the bees, the wasps, the ants apply themselves to their skilful dwellings and highly complicated economy. They are all guided with certainty by an illusion, which conceals the service of the species under the mask of an egotistical end. This probably the only way to comprehend the inner or subjective process that lies at the foundation of the manifestations of instinct.

Outwardly, however, or objectively, we find in those creatures which are to a large extent governed by instinct, especially in insects, a preponderance of the ganglion system, *i.e.*, the *subjective* nervous system, over the objective or cerebral system[12]; from which we must conclude that they are moved, not so much by objective, proper apprehension as by subjective ideas exciting desire, which arise from the influence of the ganglion system upon the brain, and accordingly by a kind of illusion; and this will be the *physiological* process in the case of all instinct. For the sake of illustration, I will mention as another example of instinct in the human species, although a weak one, the capricious appetite of women who are pregnant. It seems to arise from the fact that the nourishment of the embryo sometimes requires a special or definite modification of the blood which flows to it, upon which the food which produces such a modification at once presents itself to the pregnant woman as an object of ardent longing, thus here also an illusion arises. Accordingly woman has one instinct more than man; and the ganglion system is also much more developed in the woman. That man has fewer instincts than the brutes and that even these few can be easily led astray, may be explained from the

---

[12] Objective because it is internal to the perception of objects of the external world.

great preponderance of the brain in his case. The sense of beauty which instinctively guides the selection for the satisfaction of sexual passion is led astray when it degenerates into the tendency to pederasty; analogous to the fact that the blue-bottle (*musca vomitoria*), instead of depositing its eggs, according to instinct, in putrefying flesh, lays them in the blossom of the *Arum dracunculus*, deceived by the cadaverous smell of this plant.

Now that an instinct entirely directed to that which is to be produced lies at the foundation of all sexual love will receive complete confirmation from the fuller analysis of it, which we cannot therefore avoid. First of all we have to remark here that by nature man is inclined to inconstancy in love, woman to constancy. The love of the man sinks perceptibly from the moment it has obtained satisfaction; almost every other woman charms him more than the one he already possesses; he longs for variety. The love of the woman, on the other hand, increases just from that moment. This is a consequence of the aim of nature which is directed to the maintenance, and therefore to the greatest possible increase, of the species. The man can easily beget over a hundred children a year; the woman, on the contrary, with however many men, can yet only bring one child a year into the world (leaving twin births out of account).

Therefore the man always looks about after other women; the woman, again, sticks firmly to one man; for nature moves her, instinctively and without reflection, to retain the nourisher and protector of the future offspring. Accordingly faithfulness in marriage is with the man artificial, with the woman it is natural, and thus adultery on the part of the woman is much less pardonable than on the part of the man, both objectively on account of the consequences and also subjectively on account of its unnaturalness.[13]

But in order to be thorough and gain full conviction that the pleasure in the other sex, however objective it may seem to us, is yet merely disguised instinct, *i.e.*, sense of the species, which strives to maintain its type, we must investigate more fully the considerations which guide us in this pleasure, and enter into details of this, rarely as these details which will have to be mentioned here may have figured in a philosophical work before.[14] These considerations divide themselves into those which directly concern the type of the species, *i.e.*, beauty, those which are concerned with physical

---

[13] Schopenhauer believes he can justify by the nature the most common customs of his time.

[14] Schopenhauer is very aware of introducing in philosophy, analysis that would reveal of moralist or of psychologist, with the dangers of confusing the difference between nature and morality of the time.

qualities, and lastly, those which are merely relative, which arise from the requisite correction or neutralisation of the one-sided qualities and abnormities of the two individuals by each other. We shall go into them one by one.

The first consideration which guides our choice[15] and inclination is age. In general we accept the age from the years when menstruation begins to those when it ceases, yet we give the decided preference to the period from the eighteenth to the twenty-eighth year. Outside of these years, on the other hand, no woman can attract us: an old woman, *i.e.*, one who no longer menstruates, excites our aversion. Youth without beauty has still always attraction; beauty without youth has none. Clearly the unconscious end which guides us here is the possibility of reproduction in general: therefore every individual loses attraction for the opposite sex in proportion as he or she is removed from the fittest period for begetting or conceiving. The second consideration is that of health. Acute diseases, only temporarily disturb us, chronic diseases or cachexia[16] repel us, because they are transmitted to the child. The

---

[15] It is the choice of the masculine gender.

[16] *Cachexia*: general and deep weakness. It may be thought to be the importance in the nineteenth century of pulmonary tuberculosis (that was thought hereditary at that time). But, this disease evokes any repulsive reaction in romantic literature.

third consideration is the skeleton, because it is the basis of the type of the species. Next to age and disease nothing repels us so much as a deformed figure; even the most beautiful face can not atone for it; on the contrary, even the ugliest face when accompanied by a straight figure is unquestionably preferred. Further, we feel every disproportion of the skeleton most strongly; for example, a stunted, dumpy, short-boned figure, and many such; also a halting gait, where it is not the result of an extraneous accident. On the other hand, a strikingly beautiful figure can make up for all defects: it enchants us. Here also comes in the great value which all attach to the smallness of the feet: it depends upon the fact that they are an essential characteristic of the species, for no animal has the tarsus and the metatarsus taken together so small as man, which accords with his upright walk; he is a plantigrade. Accordingly Jesus Sirach also says "A woman with a straight figure and beautiful feet is like columns of gold in sockets of silver."[17] The teeth also are important; because they are necessary for nourishment and quite especially hereditary. The fourth condition is a certain fullness of flesh; thus a predominance of the vegetative function, of plasticity; because this promises abundant nourishment for the foetus; hence great leanness repels us in a

[17] xxvi. 23, according to the revised translation by Kraus

striking degree. A full female bosom exerts an exceptional charm upon the male sex; because, standing in direct connection with the female functions of propagation, it promises abundant nourishment to the new-born child. On the other hand, excessively fat women excite our disgust: the cause is that this indicates atrophy of the uterus, thus barrenness; which is not known by the head, but by instinct. The last consideration of all is the beauty of the face. Here also before everything else the bones are considered; therefore we look principally for a beautiful nose, and a short turned-up nose spoils everything. A slight inclination of the nose downwards or upwards has decided the happiness in life of innumerable maidens, and rightly so, for it concerns the type of the species. A small mouth, by means of small maxillae, is very essential as specifically characteristic of the human countenance, as distinguished from the muzzle of the brutes. A receding or, as it were, cut-away chin is especially disagreeable, because 'prominent chin (*mentum prominulum*)'[18] is an exclusive characteristic of our species. Finally comes the regard for beautiful eyes and forehead; it is concerned with the psychical

---

[18] Schopenhauer uses the Latin expression *mentum prominulum* of the anatomists of the time. Recall studies on the facial angle that was considered as a characteristic of the human species in the eighteenth century.

qualities, especially the intellectual which are inherited from the mother.

The unconscious considerations which, on the other hand, the inclination of women follows naturally cannot be so exactly assigned. In general the following may be asserted: They give preference to the age from thirty to thirty-five years, especially over youths who yet really present the height of human beauty. The reason is that they are not guided by taste but by instinct, which recognises in the age named the acme of reproductive power. In general they look less to beauty, especially of the face. They are principally won by the strength of the man, and the courage which is connected with this; for these promise the production of stronger children, and also a brave protector for them. Every physical defect of the man, every divergence from the type, may with regard to the child be removed by the woman in reproduction, through the fact that she herself in these respects, or even exceeds in the opposite direction. Only those qualities of the man have to be excepted which are peculiar to his sex, and which therefore the mother cannot give to the child: such are the manly structure of the skeleton, slender hips, straight bones, muscular power, courage, beard, etc. Hence it arises that women often love ugly men, but never an unmanly man, because they cannot neutralise his defects.

The second class of the considerations which lie at the foundation of sexual love are those which regard psychical qualities. Here we shall find that the woman is throughout attracted by the qualities of the heart or character in the man, as those which are inherited from the father. The woman is won especially by firmness of will, decision, and courage, and perhaps also by honesty and good-heartedness. On the other hand, intellectual gifts exercise no direct and instinctive power over her, just because they are not inherited from the father. Want of understanding does a man no harm with women; indeed extraordinary mental endowment, or even genius, might sooner influence them unfavourably as an abnormity. Hence one often sees an ugly, stupid and coarse fellow get the better of a cultured, able and amiable man with women. Also marriages from love are sometimes consummated between natures which are mentally very different: for example, the man is rough, powerful and stupid; the woman tenderly sensitive, delicately thoughtful, cultured, aesthetic, etc.; or the man is a genius and learned, the woman a goose:

"Sic visum Veneri; cui placet impares
Formas atque animos sub juga aenea
Saevo mittere cum joco"[19]

The reason is, that here quite other considerations than the intellectual predominate, — those of instinct. In marriage what is looked to is not intellectual entertainment, but the production of children: it is a bond of the heart, not of the head. It is a vain and absurd pretence when women assert that they have fallen in love with the mind of a man, or else it is the over-straining of a degenerate nature. Men, on the other hand, are not determined in their instinctive love by the qualities of the character of the woman; hence so many Socrateses have found their Xantippes[20]; for example, Shakespeare, Albrecht Durer, Byron, &c. The intellectual qualities, however, certainly influence here, because they are inherited from the mother. Yet their influence is easily outweighed by that of physical beauty, which acts directly, as concerning a more essential point. However, it happens, either from the feeling or the experience of that influence, that mothers have their daughters taught the fine arts, languages, and so forth in order to make them attractive to men, whereby they wish to assist the intellect by artificial means, just as, in case of need, they assist the hips and

---

[19] "Venus wants it as well; she likes a cruel game to put bodies and disparate minds under a yoke of iron." (Horace, "Carmina".)
[20] The cantankerous character of Socrates' wife is legendary.

the bosom. Observe that here we are speaking of that entirely immediate instinctive attraction from which alone love properly so called grows. That a woman of culture and understanding prizes understanding and intellect in a man, that a man from rational reflection should test and have regard to the character of his bride, has nothing to do with the matter with which we are dealing here. Such things lie at the bottom of a rational choice in marriage, but not of the passionate love, which is our theme.

Hitherto I have only taken account of the *absolute* considerations[21], *i.e.*, those which hold good for every one: I come now to the *relative* considerations, which are individual, because in their case what is looked to is the rectification of the type of the species, which is already defectively presented, the correction of the divergences from it which the chooser's person already bears in itself, and thus the return to the pure presentation of the type. Here, then, each one loves what he lacks. Starting from the individual constitution, and directed to the individual constitution, the choice which rests upon such relative considerations is much more definite, decided, and exclusive, than that which

---

[21] Schopenhauer uses the term "absolute" rather loosely as the simple opposition to "relative".

proceeds merely from the absolute considerations; therefore the source of really passionate love will lie, as a rule, in these relative considerations, and only that of the ordinary and slighter inclination in the absolute considerations. Accordingly it is not generally precisely correct and perfect beauties that kindle great passions. For such a truly passionate inclination to arise something is required which can only be expressed by a chemical metaphor: two persons must neutralise each other, like acid and alkali, to a neutral salt. The essential conditions demanded for this are the following. First: all sex is one-sided. This one-sidedness is more distinctly expressed in one individual than in another; therefore in every individual it can be better supplemented and neutralised by one than by another individual of the opposite sex, for each one requires a one-sidedness which is the opposite of his own to complete the type of humanity in the new individual that is to be produced, the constitution of which is always the goal toward which all tends. Physiologists know that manhood and womanhood admit of innumerable degrees, through which the former sinks to the repulsive gynandromorphy and hypospadias, and the latter rises to the graceful androgyny[22]; from both

[22] The androgyny of some ancient statues was famous and was appreciated in the neoclassical art.

sides complete hermaphroditism can be reached, at which point those individuals who, holding the exact mean between the two sexes, can be attributed to neither, and consequently are unfit to propagate the species. Accordingly, the neutralisation of two individualities by each other, of which we are speaking, demands that the definite degree of *his* manhood shall exactly correspond to the definite degree of *her* womanhood; so that the one-sidedness of each exactly annuls that of the other. Accordingly, the most manly man will seek the most womanly woman, and *vice versa*, and in the same way every individual will seek another corresponding to him or her in degree of sex. Now how far the required relation exists between two individuals is instinctively felt by them, and, together with the other relative considerations, lies at the foundations of the higher degrees of love. While, therefore, the lovers speak pathetically of the harmony of their souls, the heart of the matter is for the most part the agreement or suitableness pointed out here with reference to the being which is to be produced and its perfection, and which is also clearly of much more importance than the harmony of their souls, which often, not long after the marriage, resolves itself into a howling discord. Now, here comes in the further relative considerations, which depend upon the fact that everyone endeavours to neutralise by means of the other his weaknesses, defects, and deviations from the type, so that they will not perpetuate themselves, or even develop into complete abnormities in the child which is to be produced. The weaker a man is as regards muscular power the more he will seek strong women; and the woman on her side will do the same. But since now a less degree of muscular power is natural and regular in the woman, women as a rule will give the preference to strong men. Further, the size is an important consideration. Little men have a decided inclination for big women, and *vice versa*; and indeed in a little man the preference for big women will be so much the more passionate if he himself was begotten by a big father, and only remains little through the influence of his mother; because he has inherited from his father the vascular system and its energy, which was able to supply a large body with blood. If, on the other hand, his father and grandfather were both little, that inclination will make itself less felt. At the foundation of the aversion of a big woman to big men lies the intention of nature to avoid too big a race, if with the strength which this could impart to them would be too weak to live long. If, however, such a woman selects a big husband, perhaps for the sake of being more presentable in society, then, as a rule, her offspring will have to atone for her folly. Further, the consideration as to the complexion is very decided. Blondes prefer dark persons, or brunettes; but the latter seldom prefer the former. The reason is, that fair hair and blue eyes are themselves a variation from the type, almost an abnormity, analogous to white mice, or at least to grey horses. In no part of the world, not even in the vicinity of the pole, are they indigenous, except in Europe, and are clearly of Scandinavian origin. I may here express my opinion in passing that the white color of the skin is not natural to man, but that by nature he has a black or brown skin, like our forefathers the Hindus; that consequently a white man has never originally sprung from the womb of nature, and that thus there is no such thing as a white race, much as this is talked of, but every white man is a faded or bleached one. Forced into the strange world, where he only exists like an exotic plant, and like this requires to winter in the hothouse, in the course of thousands of years man became white. The gipsies, an Indian race which immigrated only about four centuries ago, show the transition from the complexion of the Hindu to our own. Therefore in sexual love nature strives to return to dark hair and brown eyes as the primitive type; but the white colour of the skin has become a second nature, though not so that the brown of the Hindu repels us. Finally, each one also seeks in the particular parts of the body the corrective of his own defects and aberrations, and does so the more decidedly the more important the part is. Therefore snub-nosed individuals have an inexpressible liking for hook-noses, parrot-faces; and it is the same with regard to all other parts. Men with excessively slim, long bodies and limbs can find beauty in a body which is even beyond measure stumpy and short. The considerations with regard to temperament act in an analogous manner. Each will prefer the temperament opposed to his own; yet only in proportion as his own is decided. Whoever is himself in some respect very perfect does not indeed seek and love imperfection in this respect, but is yet more easily reconciled to it than others; because he himself insures the children against great imperfection of this part. For example, whoever is himself very white will not object to a yellow complexion; but whoever has the latter will find dazzling whiteness divinely beautiful. The rare case in which a man falls in love with a decidedly ugly woman occurs when, beside the exact harmony of the degree of sex explained above, the whole of her abnormities are precisely the opposite, and thus the corrective, of his. The love is then wont to reach a high degree.

The profound seriousness with which we consider and ponder each bodily part of the woman, and she on her part does the same, the critical scrupulosity with which we inspect a woman who begins to please us, the capriciousness of our choice, the keen attention with which the bridegroom observes his betrothed, his carefulness not to be deceived in any part, and the great value which he attaches to every excess or defect in the essential parts, all this is quite in keeping with the importance of the end. For the new being to be produced will have to bear through its whole life a similar part. For example, if the woman is only a little crooked, this may impart to her son a hump, and so in all the rest. Consciousness of all this certainly does not exist. On the contrary, every one imagines that he makes that careful selection in the interest of his own pleasure (which at bottom cannot be interested in it at all); but he makes it precisely as, under the presupposition of his own corporisation, is most in keeping with the interest of the species, to maintain the type of which as pure as possible is the secret task. The individual acts here, without knowing it, by order of something higher than itself, the species; hence the importance which it attaches to things which may and indeed must be, indifferent to itself as such.[23] There is something quite peculiar in the profound unconscious

---

[23] The originality of Schopenhauer is to focus on the choice of love and its unconscious causes. But he did not seek them, as Freud will do, in infancy, the individual history.

seriousness with which two young persons of opposite sex who see each other for the first time regard each other, in the searching and penetrating glance they cast at one another, in the careful review which all the features and parts of their respective persons have to endure. This investigating and examining is the *mediation of the genius of the species*[24] on the individual which is possible through these two and the combination of its qualities. According to the result of this mediation is the degree of their pleasure in each other and this yearning for each other. This yearning, even after it has attained a considerable degree, may be suddenly extinguished again by the discovery of something that had previously remained unobserved. In this way, then, the genius of the species mediates concerning the coming race in all who are capable of reproduction. The nature of this race is the great work with which Cupid is occupied, unceasingly active, speculating, and pondering. In comparison with the importance of his great affair, which concerns the species and all coming races, the affairs of individuals in their whole ephemeral totality are very trifling; therefore he is always ready to sacrifice these regardlessly. For he

---

[24] Passage from the psychological and empirical observation to the metaphysical interpretation. But this term "meditation" is just a manner of speaking: the will-to-live has no reason other than its own assertion.

is related to them as an immortal to mortals, and his interests to theirs as infinite to finite. Thus, in the consciousness of managing affairs of a higher kind than all those which only concern individual weal or woe, he carries them on sublimely, undisturbed in the midst of the tumult of war, or in the bustle of business life, or during the raging of a plague, and pursues them even into the seclusion of the cloister.

We have seen in the above that the intensity of love increases with its individualisation, because we have shown that the physical qualities of two individuals can be such that, for the purpose of restoring as far as possible the type of the species, the one is quite specifically and perfectly the completion or supplement of the other, which therefore desires it exclusively. Already in this case a considerable passion arises, which at once gains a nobler and more sublime appearance from the fact that it is directed toward an individual object; thus, as it were, arises at the special order of the species. For the opposite reason, the mere sexual impulse is ignoble, because without individualisation it is directed to all, and strives to maintain the species only as regards quantity, with little respect as to quality. But the individualising, and with it the intensity of the love, can reach so high a degree that without its satisfaction all the good things in the world, and even life itself, lose their value. It is then a wish which attains a vehemence that no other wish ever reaches, and therefore makes one ready for any sacrifice, and in case its fulfilment remains unalterably denied, may lead to madness or suicide. At the foundation of such an excessive passion there must lie, besides the considerations we have shown above, still others which we have not thus before our eyes[25]. We must therefore assume that here not only the corporisation, but the *will* of the man and the *intellect* of the woman are specially suitable to each other, in consequence of which a perfectly definite individual can be produced by them alone, whose existence the genius of the species has here in view, for reasons which are inaccessible to us, since they lie in the nature of the thing-in-itself. Or, to speak more exactly, the will-to-live desires here to objectify itself in a perfectly definite individual, which can only be produced by this father with this mother[26]. This metaphysical desire of the will in itself has primarily no other sphere of action in the series of existences than the

---

[25] That is to say, inaccessible to the empirical or scientific observation (physiology) that was invoked until now.

[26] It is not simply the individuation through space and time. It should be understood the opposition of the species and the individual in the world of phenomena: the individual existence is particularized by the relations of space and of time. The species is a scientific concept, but this concept is an idea, an objectification of the will. Schopenhauer says it has an "upper right" than the individual one.

hearts of the future parents, which accordingly are seized with this ardent longing, and now imagine themselves to desire on their own account what really for the present has only a purely metaphysical end, *i.e.*, an end which lies outside the series of actually existing things. Thus it is the ardent longing to enter existence of the future individual which has first become possible here, a longing which proceeds from the primary source of all being, and exhibits itself in the phenomenal world as the lofty passion of the future parents for each other, paying little regard to all that is outside itself; in fact, as an unparalleled illusion, on account of which such a lover would give up all the good things of this world to enjoy the possession of this woman, who yet can give him nothing really more than any other. That yet it is just this possession that is kept in view here is seen from the fact that even this lofty passion, like all others, is extinguished in its enjoyment — to the great astonishment of those who are possessed by it. It also becomes extinct when, through the woman having turned out barren (which, according to Hufeland, may arise from nineteen accidental constitutional defects), the real metaphysical end is frustrated; just as daily happens in millions of germs trampled under foot, in which yet the same metaphysical life principle strives for existence; for which there is no other consolation than that an infinity of space, time, and matter, and consequently inexhaustible opportunity for return, stands open to the will-to-live.

The view which is here expounded must once have been present to the mind of Theophrastus Paracelsus, even if only in a fleeting form, though he has not handled this subject, and my whole system of thought was foreign to him; for, in quite a different context and in his desultory manner, he wrote the following remarkable words[27]: *"Hi sunt, quos Deus copulavit, ut eam, quae fuit Uriae et David; quamvis ex diametro (sic enim sibi humana mens persuadebat) cum justo et legitimo matrimonio pugnaret hoc....sed propter Salomonem, QUI ALIUNDE NASCI NON POTUIT, nisi ex Bathsheba, conjuncto David semine, quamvis meretrice, conjunxit eos Deus[28]"* (*De vita longa, I. 5*).

The longing of love, the *himeros*, which the poets of all ages are unceasingly occupied with expressing in innumerable forms, and do not exhaust the subject,

---

[27] Note Schopenhauer's care to avoid confusion with little scientific conceptions of the famous alchemist doctor.

[28] « They are the ones whom God has coupled as the woman who was to Uriah and to David. This union was the opposite of a just and legitimate marriage, according to the conviction of the human mind. However, because of Solomon who could only be born of Bathsheba by the seed of David, God unites them although it was adultery. » Paracelsus of Hohenheim, alchemist, astrologer, Swiss physician born in 1495, died in 1541.

nay, cannot do it justice, this longing, which attaches the idea of endless happiness to the possession of a particular woman, and unutterable pain to the thought that this possession cannot be attained, — this longing and this pain cannot obtain their material from the wants of an ephemeral individual; but they are the signs of the spirit of the species, which sees here, to be won or lost, a means for the attainment of its ends which cannot be replaced, and therefore groans deeply. The species alone has infinite life, and therefore is capable of infinite desires, infinite satisfaction, and infinite pain. But these are here imprisoned in the narrow breast of a mortal. No wonder, then, if such a breast seems like to burst, and can find no expression for the intimations of infinite rapture or infinite misery with which it is filled. This, then, affords the materials for all erotic poetry of a sublime kind, which accordingly rises into transcendent metaphors, soaring above all that is earthly. This is the theme of Petrarch, the material for the St. Preuxs, Werthers, and Jacobo Ortis, who apart from it could not be understood nor explained. For that infinite esteem for the loved one cannot rest upon some spiritual excellences, or in general upon any objective, real qualities of hers; for one thing, because she is often not sufficiently well known to the lover, as was the case with Petrarch. The spirit of the species alone can see at one glance what *worth* she has for *it*, for its ends. And great passions also arise, as a rule, at the first glance:

"Who ever loved that loved not at first sight?"[29]

In this regard a passage in the romance of *"Guzman de Alfarache,"* by Mateo Aleman, which has been famous for 250 years, is remarkable: *"No es necessario, para que uno ame, que pasa distancia de tiempo, que siga discurso, ni haga eleccion, sino que con aquella primera y sola vista, concurran juntamente cierta correspondencia o consonancia, o lo que aca solemos vulgarmente decir, una confrontacion de sangre, a que por particular influxo suelen mover las estrellas."* (For one to love it is not necessary that much time should pass, that he should set about reflecting and make a choice; but only that at that first and only glance a certain correspondence and consonance should be encountered on both sides, or that which in common life we are wont to call a *sympathy of the blood*, and to which a special influence of the stars generally impels), P. ii. lib. iii. c. 5. Accordingly the loss of the loved one, through a rival, or through death, is also for the passionate lover a pain that surpasses all others, just because it is of a

---

[29] Shakespeare, "As you like it," III. 5.

transcendental kind, since it affects him not merely as an individual, but attacks him in his 'être éternel (*essentia aeterna*)', in the life of the species into whose special will and service he was here called. Hence jealousy is such torment and so grim, and the surrender of the loved one is the greatest of all sacrifices. A hero is ashamed of all lamentations except the lamentation of love, because in this it is not he but the species that laments. In Calderon's "Zenobia the Great" there is in the first act a scene between Zenobia and Decius in which the latter says:

> *"(Cielos, luego tu me quieres?*
> *Perdiera cien mil victorias,*
> *Volvierame),*[30]*"* etc.

Here, honour, which hitherto outweighed every interest, is beaten out of the field as soon as sexual love, *i.e.*, the interest of the species, comes into play, and sees before it a decided advantage; for this is infinitely superior to every interest of mere individuals, however important it may be. Therefore to this alone honour, duty, and fidelity yield after they have withstood every

[30] "Heavens! then you love me? For this I would sacrifice a thousand victories, […]."

other temptation, including the threat of death. In the same way we find in private life that conscientiousness is in no point so rare as in this: it is here sometimes set aside even by persons who are otherwise honest and just, and adultery is recklessly committed when passionate love, *i.e.*, the interest of the species, has mastered them. It even seems as if in this they believed themselves to be conscious of a higher right than the interests of individuals can ever confer; just because they act in the interest of the species. In this reference Chamfort's remark is worth noticing: *"Quand un homme et une femme ont l'un pour l'autre une passion violente, il me semble toujours que quelque soient les obstacles qui les séparent, un mari, des parents, etc., les deux amants sont l'un a l'autre, de par la Nature, qu'ils s'appartiennent de droit divin, malgré les lois et les conventions humaines.[31]"* Whoever is inclined to be incensed at this should be referred to the remarkable indulgence which the Savior shows in the Gospel to the woman taken in adultery, in the He also assumes the same guilt in the case of all present. From this point of view the greater part of the "Decameron" appears as

---

[31] "When a man and a woman have for each other a violent passion, it always seems that whatever obstacles that separate them, husband, parents, etc.., the two lovers are one to another, by nature, they belong to divine right, despite laws and human conventions."

mere mocking and jeering of the genius of the species at the rights and interests of individuals which it tramples under foot. Differences of rank and all similar circumstances, when they oppose the union of passionate lovers, are set aside with the same ease and treated as nothing by the genius of the species, which, pursuing its ends that concern innumerable generations, blows off as spray such human laws and scruples. From the same deep-lying grounds, when the ends of passionate love are concerned, every danger is willingly encountered, and those who are otherwise timorous here become courageous. In plays and novels also we see, with ready sympathy, the young persons who are fighting the battle of their love, *i.e.*, the interest of the species, gain the victory of their elders, who are thinking only of the welfare of the individuals[32]. For the efforts of the lovers appear to us as much more important, sublime, and therefore right, than anything that can be opposed to them, as the species is more important than the individual. Accordingly the fundamental theme of almost all comedies is the appearance of the genius of the species with its aims, which are opposed to the personal interest of the individuals presented, and therefore threaten to

---

[32] Here social conventions are an integral part of individual interests (relative to those of the species).

undermine their happiness. As a rule it attains its end, which, as in accordance with poetical justice, satisfies the spectator, because he feels that the aims of the species are much to be preferred to those of the individual. Therefore at the conclusion he leaves the victorious lovers quite confidently, because he shares with them the illusion that they have founded their own happiness, against the will and foresight of their elders. In has been attempted in single, abnormal comedies to reverse the matter and bring about the happiness of the individuals at the cost of the aims of the species; but then the spectator feels the pain which the genius of the species suffers, and is not consoled by the advantages which are thereby assured to the individuals. As examples of this kind two very well-known little pieces occur to me: *"La reine de seize ans,"* and *"La marriage de raison."*[33] In tragedies concerning love affairs, since the aims of the species are frustrated, the lovers who were its tools, generally perish also; for example, in "Romeo and Juliet," "Tancred," "Don Carlos," "Wallenstein," "The Bride of Messina,"[34] and many others.

---

[33] Two comedies of 1820 and 1826 of Eugène Scribe (1791-1861), today completely forgotten, but who took a long carrier of bestselling author thanks to the ability to his intrigues.

[34] We recognize successively the Shakespeare's tragedy, a tragedy of Voltaire ("Tancredi") and three pieces of Friedrich Schiller.

The love of a man often affords comical, and also tragical phenomena; both because, taken possession of by the spirit of the species, he is now ruled by this, and no longer belongs to himself: his conduct thereby becomes unsuited to the individual. That which in the higher grades of love imparts such a tinge of poetry and sublimeness to his thoughts, which gives them even a transcendental and hyperphysical tendency[35], on account of which he seems to lose sight altogether of his real, very physical aim, is at bottom this, that he is now inspired by the spirit of the species whose affairs are infinitely more important than all those which concern mere individuals, in order to found under the special direction of this spirit the whole existence of an indefinitely long posterity with this individual and exactly determined nature, which it can only receive from him as father and the woman he loves as mother, and which otherwise could never, *as such*, attain to existence, while the objectification of the will-to-live expressly demands that existence. It is the feeling that he is acting in affairs of such transcendent importance which raises the lover so high above everything earthly, nay, even above himself, and gives such a hyperphysical clothing to his very physical desires, that love becomes a

[35] The terms "transcendent" and "hyperphysical" ironically refer to the romantic illusion. But this illusion has nevertheless a metaphysical meaning.

poetical episode even in the life of the most prosaic man; in which last case the matter sometimes assumes a comical aspect. The mandate of the will which objectifies itself in the species exhibits itself in the consciousness of the lover under the mask of the anticipation of an infinite blessedness which is to be found for him in the union with this female individual. Now, in the highest grade of love the chimera becomes so radiant that if it cannot be attained life itself loses all charm, and now appears so joyless, hollow, and insupportable that the disgust at it even overcomes the fear of death, so that it is then sometimes voluntarily cut short. The will of such a man has been caught in the vortex of the will of the species, or this has obtained such a great predominance over the individual will that if such a man cannot be effective in the first capacity, he disdains to be so in the last. The individual is here too weak a vessel to be capable of enduring the infinite longing of the will of the species concentrated upon a definite object. No year passes without proving the reality of what has been expounded by several cases of all these kinds.

Not only, however, has the unsatisfied passion of love sometimes a tragic issue, but the satisfied passion also leads oftener to unhappiness than to happiness. For its demands often conflict so much with the personal welfare of him who is concerned that they undermine it, because they are incompatible with his other circumstances, and disturb the plan of life built upon them. Nay, not only with external circumstances is love often in contradiction, but even with the lover's own individuality, for it flings itself upon persons who, apart from the sexual relation, would be hateful, contemptible, and even abhorrent to the lover. But so much more powerful is the will of the species than that of the individual that the lover shuts his eyes to all those qualities which are repellent to him, overlooks all, ignores all, and binds himself forever to the object of his passion — so entirely is he blinded by that illusion, which vanishes as soon as the will of the species is satisfied, and leaves behind a detested companion for life. Only from this can it be explained that we often see very reasonable and excellent men bound to termagants and she-devils, and cannot conceive how they could have made such a choice. On this account the ancients represented love as blind. Indeed, a lover may even know distinctly and feel bitterly the faults of temperament and character of his bride, which promise him a miserable life, and yet not be frightened away: —

> "I ask not, I care not,
> If guilt's in thy heart.

I know that I love thee
Whatever thou art."[36]

For ultimately he seeks not his own things, but those of a third person, who has yet to come into being, although he is involved in the illusion that what he seeks is his own affair. But it is just this not seeking of one's own things which is everywhere the stamp of greatness, that gives to passionate love also a touch of sublimity, and makes it a worthy subject of poetry. Finally, sexual love is compatible even with the extremes hate toward its object: therefore Plato has compared it to the love of the wolf for the sheep[37]. This case appears when a passionate lover, in spite of all efforts and entreaties, cannot obtain a favourable hearing on any condition: —

"I love her and hate her."[38]

The hatred of the loved one which then is kindled sometimes goes so far that the lover murders her, and

---

[36] This poem is taken from *Irish Melodies* of the Irish poet Thomas Moore.

[37] A kind of proverb, quoted by Plato in "Phaedrus".

[38] Shakespeare, Cymbeline, iii. 5.

then himself. One or two examples of this generally happen every year; they will be found in the newspapers. Therefore Goethe's lines are quite correct: —

"By all despised love! By hellish element!
Would that I knew a worse, that I might swear by!"[39]

It is really no hyperbole if a lover describes the coldness of his beloved and the delight of her vanity, which feeds on his sufferings, as cruelty; for he is under the influence of an impulse which, akin to the instinct of insects, compels him, in spite of all grounds of reason, to pursue his end unconditionally, and to undervalue everything else: he cannot give it up. Not one but many a Petrarch has there been who was compelled to drag through life the unsatisfied ardor of love, like a fetter, an iron weight at his foot, and breathe his sighs in lonely woods[40]; but only in the one Petrarch

---

[39] "Bei aller verschmähten Liebe ! beim höllischen Elemente!
Ich wollt', ich wüsst' was ärger's, dass ich fluchen könnte."
(Goethe, *Faust*)
"By all that ever was jilted! By all the infernal fires!
I wish I knew something worse, to curse as my heart desires!"
(Goethe, "Faust")

[40] The latter image is characteristic of Petrarchism. Pétrarque

dwelt also the gift of poetry; so that Goethe's beautiful lines hold good of him: —

"And when in misery the man was dumb
A god gave me the power to tell my sorrow."[41]

In fact, the genius of the species wages war throughout with the guardian geniuses of individuals, is their pursuer and enemy, always ready relentlessly to destroy personal happiness in order to carry out its ends; nay, the welfare of whole nations has sometimes been sacrificed to its humours. An example of this is given us by Shakespeare in "Henry VI.", pt. iii., act 3, sc. 2 and 3. All this depends on the fact that the species, as that in which the root of our being lies, has a closer and earlier right to us than the individual; hence its affairs take precedence. From the feeling of this the ancients personified the genius of the species in Cupid, a malevolent, cruel, and therefore ill-reputed god, in spite of his childish appearance; a capricious, despotic demon[42], but yet lord of gods and men:

---

composed very famous sonnets and the "Il Canzoniere" (Song Book) in honor of Laura whom he had only seen at Avignon in 1327. He marked the love poetry up to the Romantism.
[41] Goethe, *Torquato Tasso* (tragedy), V, 5.
[42] The demon in Greek mythology is not the lord of Hell, but a

"Su, do theos turanne k'anthropos, Eros!"[43]
(*Tu, deorum hominumque tyranne, Amor!*)

A deadly shot, blindness, and wings are his attributes. The latter signify inconstancy; and this appears, as a rule, only with the disillusion which is the consequence of satisfaction.

Because the passion depended upon an illusion, which represented that which has only value for the species as valuable for the individual, the deception must vanish after the attainment of the end of the species. The spirit of the species which took possession of the individual sets it free again. Forsaken by this spirit, the individual falls back into its original limitation and narrowness, and sees with wonder that after such a high, heroic, and infinite effort nothing has resulted for its pleasure but what every sexual gratification affords. Contrary to expectation, it finds itself no happier than before. It observes that it has been the dupe of the will of the species. Therefore, as a rule, a

---

kind of intermediary between the divine and the human. This is the status of love in Plato's "Symposium".

[43] *"Love, you tyrant of gods and men!"* — This verse is of the "Andromeda" of Euripides (lost tragedy)

Theseus who has been made happy will forsake his Ariadne. If Petrarch's passion had been satisfied, his song would have been silenced from that time forth, like that of the bird as soon as the eggs are laid.

Here let me remark in passing that however much my metaphysics of love will displease the very persons who are entangled in this passion, yet if rational considerations in general could avail anything against it, the fundamental truth disclosed to me would necessarily fit one more than anything else to subdue it. But the saying of the old comedian will, no doubt, remain true: *"Quae res in se neque consilium, neque modum habet ullum, eam consilio regere non potes."*[44]

Marriages from love are made in the interest of the species, not of the individuals. Certainly the persons concerned imagine they are advancing their own happiness; but their real end is one which is foreign to themselves, for it lies in the production of an individual which is only possible through them. Brought together by this aim, they ought henceforth to try to get on together as well as possible. But very often the pair brought together by that instinctive illusion, which is

---

[44] "You cannot govern by reason of something (= the woman) that has in itself neither reason nor measure". Terence, "Eunuch".

the essence of passionate love, will, in other respects, be of very different natures. This comes to light when the illusion vanishes, as it necessarily must. Accordingly love marriages, as a rule, turn out unhappy; for through them the coming generation is cared for at the expense of the present. "*Quien se casa por amores, ha de vivir con dolores*" (Who marries for love must live in sorrow), says the Spanish proverb. The opposite is the case with marriages contracted for purposes of convenience, generally in accordance with the choice of the parents. The considerations prevailing here, of whatever kind they may be, are at least real, and cannot vanish of themselves. Through them, however, the happiness of the present generation is certainly cared for, to the disadvantage of the coming generation, and notwithstanding this it remains problematical. The man who in his marriage looks to money more than to the satisfaction of his inclination lives more in the individual than in the species; which is directly opposed to the truth; hence it appears unnatural, and excites a certain contempt. A girl who, against the advice of her parents, rejects the offer of a rich and not yet old man, in order, setting aside all considerations of convenience, to choose according to her instinctive inclination alone, sacrifices her individual welfare to the species. But just on this account one cannot withhold from her a certain approbation; for she has preferred what is of most importance, and has acted in the spirit of nature (more exactly, of the species), while the parents advised in the spirit of individual egoism[45]. In accordance with all this, it appears as if in making a marriage either the individual or the interests of the species must come off a loser. And this is generally the case; for that convenience and passionate love should go hand in hand is the rarest of lucky accidents. The physical, moral, or intellectual deficiency of the nature of most men may to some extent have its ground in the fact that marriages are ordinarily entered into not from pure choice and inclination, but from all kinds of external considerations, and on account of accidental circumstances. If, however, beside convenience, inclination is also to a certain extent regarded, this is, as it were, an agreement with the genius of the species. Happy marriages are well known to be rare; just because it lies in the nature of marriage that its chief end is not the present but the coming generation. However, let me add, for the consolation of tender, loving natures, that sometimes passionate sexual love associates itself with a feeling of an entirely different origin — real friendship based upon agreement of disposition, which yet for the

---

[45] Conveniences and social life in general result from the conflicts of selfishness.

most part only appears when sexual love proper is extinguished in its satisfaction. This friendship will the generally spring from the fact that the supplementing and corresponding physical, moral, and intellectual qualities of the two individuals, from which sexual love arose, with reference to the child to be produced, are, with reference also to the individuals themselves, related to each other in a supplementary manner as opposite qualities of temperament and mental gifts, and thereby form the basis of a harmony of disposition.

The whole metaphysics of love here dealt with stands in close connection with my metaphysics in general, and the light which it throws upon this may be summed up as follows.

We have seen that the careful selection for the satisfaction of the sexual impulse, a selection which rises through innumerable degrees up to that of passionate love, depends on the highly serious interest which man takes in the special personal constitution of the next generation. Now this exceedingly remarkable interest confirms two truths which have been set forth in the preceding chapters.

(1.) The indestructibility of the true nature of man, which lives on in that coming generation. For that interest which is so lively and eager, and does not spring from reflection and intention, but from the inmost characteristics and tendencies of our nature, could not be so indelibly present and exercise such great power over man if he were absolutely perishable, and were merely followed in time by a race actually and entirely different from him.

(2.) That his true nature lies more in the species than in the individual. For that interest in the special nature of the species, which is the root of all love, from the passing inclination to the serious passion, is for everyone really the highest concern, the success or failure of which touches him most sensibly; therefore it is called *par excellence* the affair of the heart. Moreover, when this interest has expressed itself strongly and decidedly, everything which merely concerns one's own person is postponed and necessarily sacrificed to it. Through this, then, man shows that the species lies closer to him than the individual, and he lives more immediately in the former than in the latter. Why does the lover hang with complete abandonment on the eyes of his chosen one, and is ready to make every sacrifice for her? Because it is his immortal part that longs after her; while it is only his mortal part that desires everything else. That vehement or intense longing directed to a particular woman is accordingly an immediate pledge of the indestructibility of the kernel of our being, and of its continued existence in the species. But to regard this continued existence as something trifling and insufficient is an error which arise from the fact that under the conception of the continued life of the species one think nothing more than the future existence of beings similar to us, but in no regard identical with us; and this again because, starting from knowledge directed towards without, one takes into consideration only the external form of the species as we apprehend it in perception, and not its inner nature. But it is just this inner nature which lies at the foundation of our own consciousness as its kernel, and hence indeed is more immediate than this itself, and as thing-in-itself, free from the Principle of individuation (*pricipium individuationis*), is really the same and identical in all individuals, whether they exist together or after each other. Now this is the will to live, thus just that which desires life and continuance so vehemently. This accordingly is spared and unaffected by death. It can attain to no better state than its present one; and consequently for it, with life, the constant suffering and striving of the individuals is certain. To free it from this is reserved for the denial of the will to live, as the means by which the individual breaks away from the stem of the species, and surrenders that existence in it. We lack conceptions for that which it now is; indeed all data for such conceptions are wanting. We can only describe it as that which is free to be will-to-live or not. Buddhism denotes the latter case by the word Nirvana. It is the point which remains for ever unattainable to all human knowledge, just as such.

If now, from the standpoint of this last consideration, we contemplate the turmoil of life, we behold all occupied with its want and misery, straining all their powers to satisfy its infinite needs and to ward off its multifarious sorrows, yet without daring to hope anything else than simply the preservation of this tormented existence for a short span of time. In between, however, in the midst of the tumult, we see the glances of two lovers meet longingly; yet why so secretly, fearfully, and stealthily? Because the lovers are the traitors who seek to perpetuate the whole want and drudgery, which would otherwise speedily reach an end; this they wish to frustrate, as others like them have frustrated it before.

Printed in Great Britain
by Amazon